UnSweetined

JODIE SWEETIN

with Jon Warech

unSweetined

G

GALLERY BOOKS

NEW YORK LONDON TORONTO SYDNEY

Gallery Books
A Division of Simon & Schuster, Inc.
1230 Avenue of the Americas
New York, NY 10020

First Gallery Books trade paperback edition July 2010

GALLERY BOOKS and colophon are trademarks of
Simon & Schuster, Inc.

For information about special discounts for bulk purchases,
please contact Simon & Schuster Special Sales at 1-866-506-1949
or business@simonandschuster.com.

The Simon & Schuster Speakers Bureau can bring authors to your
live event. For more information or to book an event contact the
Simon & Schuster Speakers Bureau at 1-866-248-3049 or visit our
website at www.simonspeakers.com.

Manufactured in the United States of America

20 19 18 17 16 15 14 13 12 11

Library of Congress Catologing-in-Publication Data is available.

ISBN 978-1-4391-5268-3
ISBN 978-1-4391-5269-0 (pbk)
ISBN 978-1-4391-5820-3 (ebook)

*To my family for loving me
through it all*

CONTENTS

PREFACE

Before you dive into this book, before you read about my life, before you judge me from the stories you may have already heard, there are a few things you should know. First and foremost I am a recovering drug addict and alcoholic. By recovering, I mean that I battle with my disease every single day. I am constantly going to meetings, talking with sober friends, and doing whatever it takes to stay sober.

As of the day I turned in this manuscript—April 1, 2009—I am 114 days sober. If you do the math in your head, then yes, I relapsed since I started writing this book sober in October. I was on location for a movie and I drank. You'll read all about it.

I mention it now so you can understand where I am coming from while you read this book. I'm not an eighty-year-old woman reflecting on my life and sharing stories from decades ago. I'm telling you the story of what brought me to where I am now. Right now. Today.

I can't go out and have one drink. That's one of the hardest things for me to be able to say. When friends want to go to dinner and get drinks, I turn them down. The minute I take that first sip, I need the whole bottle. So I stay away. I hang out with people who are sober and have been for years. Staying sober is what is important to me. That's all that matters.

I've been humbled enough that my pride will not get in the way of my sobriety. If it takes hanging out only with people who don't drink or bringing a sober babysitter along on, say, a book tour, then that's what I'm going to do. I'm not ashamed. I'm willing to do whatever it takes. Whatever uncomfortable situation I may need to endure to make this work, I will do it.

Part of recovery is sitting down, looking at your character defects—the destructive things that you do over and over again—and resolving to change them. As I've written down all my experiences, I've had the chance to really look at everything and to ask myself, how can I change? I know that I'm working on it. I'm a work in progress.

Each story and each experience has made me who I am today. I truly believe that I'm a stronger person and a better mother for all of it. My life, for better or worse, led me down a path that threw me into adulthood at age five and again at age nineteen. Now, at age twenty-seven, I'm finally ready for it, and as far as I'm concerned, the third time is the charm; Zoie, my beautiful daughter, has a mother who is at the right place in her life to be the best mother she can be.

This book was difficult to write. It's scary to have to examine yourself, especially knowing some of the roads you've traveled. I don't think anyone relishes the idea of recounting all the things they've done wrong or replaying every mistake they've made.

Of course there are certain things that I'm not going to mention publicly, things that I'm too horrified to tell anyone. Trust me, though, you'll get the point. This book is a huge step for me in being honest and open and not hiding anything.

My whole life used to be about appearances and about caring what other people thought. For the addict, it's a cycle that keeps repeating itself: you're self-conscious, so you drink or use to cover it up, but in doing so, you end up acting like a complete asshole. Everything you feared would happen, happens. It becomes a self-fulfilling prophecy and in the end, for me, it not only damaged everyone's opinion of me, but also hurt a number of people along the way.

Being honest with myself is probably one of the hardest things that I have to do every day. Since I was a little girl, I've felt that there are different sides to me and I've never told anybody—not even myself—the whole truth about who I actually am. I was never just Jodie. I was always trying to be different things, to be someone else. Now, every day that I'm sober, it gets a lot harder to lie to myself and others, to keep up the persona created once upon a time for a fictional character named Stephanie Tanner. The honesty, though, is invigorating. It feels great to put this out there, to end the lies, and to close the book on my troubled past.

I finally feel like I can live out loud, without being afraid of my past and the skeletons that exist there. I can be comfortable in my own skin. I have nothing to hide. I'm not scared anymore. This is my life.

While this is a book about recovery, I am by no means an expert in sobriety. When I speak at colleges, I always say, "I'm not here to tell you not to do drugs or not to drink." That is not my purpose at those speeches, or now with this book. I know from experience that being told not to do something is not going to do a damn bit of good. It doesn't do any good when you're told by your family, let alone some actress.

This is the story of my life, what I went through, and where I am now. This is what happened to me and how I felt about it. Maybe it will make you reflect on some of your own decisions and maybe it won't. Either way, it's not, by any means, a guide on how to get your life together. I hope you can read this and have a little understanding and empathy for what people in my situation go through. My life has been a series of good and bad, funny and sad, happy and tragic. I don't plan to use this book to teach some sort of lesson on life, except that we are all human and we all make mistakes and more mistakes and sometimes the same mistakes, but eventually we learn from them.

I look at this time in my life as a second chance. By reading this book you are letting me know you're rooting for me.

Ultimately though, this book is about finally loving myself. It's not about worrying what you think. It's about growing comfortable in my own skin. It's about my life and coming to terms with my choices. The more I think about it, the more I realize that writing this book was an important part in making that happen.

unSweetined

chapter one

SPEECH IMPEDIMENT

fuck it.

I was tired of trying. Tired of controlling myself. Tired of caring.

It was a Sunday night and my options were to sit home and get some rest for the big day I had on Monday or to go out, party, and not worry about anything. So when a friend called and asked me if I wanted to head to Hermosa Beach, I didn't hesitate.

Before I knew it I was smoking meth and doing my hair, preparing for a big night. I drove off solo with my to-go cup filled with alcohol. I never went anywhere without my to-go cup.

It was a typical night of partying. I met some people at a bar in Hermosa Beach that played house music on Sundays from 2:00 p.m. until around 2:00 a.m. I was friendly with the bar's owner so there was always a table waiting for me, and half-priced bottles for being such a good customer.

From the second I walked in, it was on. Some friend gave me a hug and put Ecstasy right in my mouth. That's how the night started. Simple as that.

Coke. No problem. We were doing it right at the table. Meth wasn't as socially acceptable so I did that at home, alone, or with a couple friends who were also using. But the coke, the Ecstasy—the party—went until closing. It almost always did.

Then it was back to my place in Westchester, a Los Angeles neighborhood around the corner from LAX. It was always back to my place. Somehow the group had grown to about fifteen or twenty people. I was playing the role of after-party host. Looking back, I think I liked the control. I was always the driver, the host; it was always my show. With people waiting to party, I went into the kitchen and returned with a bottle of Jack Daniel's in one hand, a bottle of champagne under my arm, and a big plate of coke in the other hand for all of my guests. The crowd went wild. Standing ovation. Just how I liked it.

As usual the party continued into the near-daylight hours. There was still a plate of coke on the living-room table and a handful of friends—and I use that term loosely—were making themselves at home.

The only problem? In seven hours I would be standing in front of a roomful of college students at Marquette University telling them how great it felt to overcome a drug addiction and how important it was to stay off drugs. I had a flight to catch and needed to be at the airport by 5:30 a.m., and at a quarter to five, I was still nose-deep in a pile of cocaine with a roomful of strangers listening to house music. And I hadn't even packed!

I was pretty good at pulling off this kind of thing. All my life I had given everyone exactly what they wanted. If *Full House* producers needed someone to look cute while eating Oat Boats, I smiled in my cereal. If my friends needed a house to party in, I opened my doors, supplied drugs, and broke up lines of cocaine with a credit card. And if America decided I was supposed to be a role model, I hopped on a plane, turned on my best Stephanie-Tanner-all-grown-up face-and gave a speech.

So at 5:00 a.m. I threw some clothes in a bag, probably forgetting socks or toothpaste or something important, and attempted to make a clean escape. But the night of partying really left me frazzled. I came into the living room with my packed bag in hand and started shaking. I couldn't speak. I couldn't think. I had been up for two days straight, partying without a care in the world, and now I was starting to lose it.

On the car ride I realized I was wearing a T-shirt that said "Things you shouldn't take to the airport" with pictures of drugs, guns, and a toothpaste tube larger than three ounces. I was one for three; I was carrying a bag of cocaine because I knew I couldn't get through the next twenty-four hours without it—and praying the stupid shirt didn't give me away to the airport security guard. That sort of paranoia comes along with drug use. *The guard searching my bag will not see the humor in my T-shirt and will look extra hard through my bags. Oh my God! What am I going to do?*

He did search pretty hard, but not because of the shirt. I took a deep breath and attempted to remain cool as the guard rummaged through my belongings. My friend who drove me to the airport told me I probably shouldn't talk to anybody because at that point I couldn't put together a complete sentence. The security guy took out my cosmetic case and asked me about every item. It took every ounce of energy I had to get out the words "lip gloss" and "mascara" without looking like a complete wreck. But I was dying inside. I thought this was it. I was going to get busted. How could I not? The guard then pulled out the compact where I kept my coke. My heart was beating through my chest. I thought for sure I was going to be arrested. And then it happened . . .

"OK, ma'am, have a nice flight."

I was safe.

I sat down at the gate and nearly broke down. What am I doing? What the hell is wrong with me? How did I become this person?

If I had had that gun my shirt warned against, I probably would have blown my brains out. I was miserable . . . and exhausted.

When I got to my hotel near Marquette University in Milwaukee, Wisconsin, I slept for a few hours but when I woke up I was still dead tired. I was a mess. Luckily I had the coke to pick me back up. I did a few key bumps and headed to the lecture hall, where a sold-out crowd waited to hear me speak. I thought for sure that one of the professors would take one look at me and kick me out. But none did. They wanted to hear about the trials and tribulations of Jodie Sweetin, or at least the Jodie Sweetin I had created by appearing on *Good Morning America* and talking to *People* magazine.

I stood up at the podium, looked around the room, and put on my best TV smile. I was so disappointed in myself. I was living a complete lie. But unfortunately, guilt doesn't make you stop. I talked about growing up on television and about how great my life was now that I was sober, and then midspeech I started to cry. The crowd probably thought that the memories of hitting rock bottom were too much for me to handle. Or maybe they thought the tears were just a way for an actor to send a message that drugs are bad. I don't know what they thought.

I know what they didn't think. They didn't think I was coming down from a two-day bender of coke, meth, and Ecstasy and they didn't think that I was lying to them with every sentence that came out of my mouth. That much I do know. The little bit of coke that I had done before the speech wasn't enough to make me forget how bad I felt for doing what I was doing. The guilt was eating away at me. I was struggling to keep it together, but no one realized that. I finished. They applauded. Standing ovation. Just how I liked it. And it was over.

I was just so tired. Tired of lying. Tired of pretending to

be someone that I wasn't. I took a deep breath and walked out of the lecture hall. I went back to my hotel room and buried my face in my hands. I couldn't keep doing this. It had to end.

But not today. I wiped away the tears and finished the baggie of coke.

Fuck it. I'll quit tomorrow.

It had been a year since I went on *Good Morning America* and told the world that I was a recovered drug addict. And back then I really was recovering—or trying to, anyway. I had been sober for a few months, but I knew in the back of my mind it wasn't over. I wasn't ready.

But the story was a good one and it landed me the speaking jobs I needed to keep my career going and the drug money rolling in. Drugs and alcohol don't come cheap—especially when you are also buying for a group of friends who mooch off your residual checks. I didn't put up with eight seasons of Kimmy Gibbler so *they* could get high!

With the new income and a new house in Los Angeles it was all too easy to get right back into drugs.

It started one day, just a few months after my *GMA* spot, when I got a random phone call from a friend who I used with and who occasionally sold me drugs. I invited her to my place. I was in an apartment at the time. I knew it was a really bad idea to invite her over but I wanted to test myself,

I guess. We hung out, played cards. I told her I hadn't done meth in a while. One thing led to another and just like that, I was back.

After trying to stay sober and then relapsing a number of times, battling the decision to remain sober for a couple of months, I began to give up on myself. Then, when I moved into the house, I stopped putting in the effort altogether. "You can do this again," I told myself about using. I wasn't in a relationship and I didn't have a good group of friends around me. I was frustrated and tired of trying. I had it in my head that I just wasn't done.

I was always up for any party, especially if it involved Las Vegas, but my newfound careless attitude often got in my way. I regularly lost cell phones, wallets, and other valu-ables. One weekend, everyone decided to head out to Vegas, but before I could leave, I had to get cash from the bank since I had misplaced my ATM card. I took out ten thousand dollars in cash to bring with me to bankroll the alcohol and drugs for everyone, as usual, and a little shop-ping for me.

In Sin City I spent two thousand dollars on makeup and an outfit for the evening and was ready to have fun. The night brought us to various clubs and then to a blow-out back at the hotel. Random people made their way in and out of my party until the sun came up. The next morning I noticed that the remaining eight thousand dol-lars was gone. Maybe I lost it, or maybe it was stolen. I didn't care.

Whether in Vegas or in Hollywood, people would call

and ask if I had plans, and even when I had had no intention
of going out, I would say, "yeah sure" and it would be off to a
night on the town. Outside of the speeches, I didn't have any
responsibilities so I often blew off my family and sober
friends and opted to hang out with whoever wanted to do
drugs.

Quickly, I was back to partying like I was at my worst,
spending seven hundred dollars a week on meth, coke, and
Ecstasy and another four to five thousand dollars every
week or two on table service at various Hollywood hot
spots. After partying, I'd head to random colleges and give
speeches that were packed with lies. If during the Q & A
portion someone asked me how long I had been sober, I'd
say I had gotten out of rehab in April 2005, and out of
sober living in October that same year. That part was
true—but I was covering up my relapses. I felt terrible
about what I was doing. I thought that maybe, if I kept getting up there, giving these talks, and saying I was sober
enough that eventually it would happen for me: The story I
was telling, with the happy ending I was creating, would
somehow come true.

But even with my life as messy as it was, I hadn't really
hit rock bottom yet. I was too strong to hit that sort of low. I
wasn't going to overdose, wind up in the hospital, or have
any near-death scares like I did the first time around. I was
too in control.

It was a far cry from the cute little girl that everyone remembered from *Full House*—the girl everyone expected
me to be for the rest of my life. I wasn't Stephanie Tanner

or the girl I was pretending to be in speeches and interviews, but I wasn't exactly the drug addict, wild child that
my friends thought I was either. I didn't know who I was.
That was the problem that may have led to my drug use in
the first place, a problem that goes back as far as I can remember. . . .

chapter two

LET THERE BE LIGHTS, CAMERA, ACTION

there is no business like show business, as they say, and I knew that at a very young age. Before Mary-Kate and Ashley Olsen were born, before my first "How rude!", before John Stamos's mullet went prime time, I hit the stage at age three for a nursery school dance recital, and I stole the show.

When I say I stole the show, I mean I *stole* the show. Even with a dozen or so three-year-olds dressed like Cabbage Patch Kids dancing onstage, the minute I stepped out there, I had arrived.

We were supposed to walk out in a straight line, but I ignored the other girls and worked my way to the front. I immediately started doing my own thing—turning around in the opposite direction, busting out my own little sequence, and pushing girls out of the way—because, you know, they didn't know what they were doing and I needed to be center stage.

It was then that my mom, Janice, thought, "Maybe she should be on TV." I was a natural. While the other kids were terrified onstage, I was smiling, loving every minute of the attention, owning the audience. I thrived on the attention, the spotlight.

My mom realized that I came alive while performing. She helped me get involved in all sorts of performing arts, from recitals and the occasional play or puppet show (put on for my family or anyone who would watch), to beauty pageants (though I was no JonBenét Ramsey—just a little lip gloss and mascara and I did my thing).

Although I had fun and did well in pageants, I wanted more. I told my mom I wanted to be a "modeler," my name for actors on TV. By the age of four I could read and memorize lines and I was constantly performing. I even had this little harmonica I carried with me everywhere—it was always showtime!

I took direction well, so my mom decided to cautiously test the Hollywood waters. "Just a few commercial auditions and that's it!" my mom exclaimed when I begged for more than the pageants. Her casual, let's-not-go-crazy-here plan immediately led to an Oscar Mayer hot dog commercial.

Hollywood, it turned out, loved me. I'd audition for one commercial and land a totally different, bigger commercial, or I'd go on set for a commercial and wind up taking the other kids' jobs because I had done so well.

Early on, everything just fell into my lap. There was

nothing but success, and everything seemed perfect. In the beginning, all was good.

I was enjoying acting, and more important, I didn't see it as work. Acting gig after acting gig came my way, and my hobby turned into a full-time operation. My parents saw how much I loved it, so my mom started officially managing me: taking me to auditions, acting classes, and singing lessons.

My mom loved it, not because she saw fame and fortune but because she loved being with me and watching over me. Plus, she was a big fan of dress up. I had an outfit for every occasion, from Easter Sunday to regular airplane rides. My hair was always done, my socks matched my shoes, and I was perfectly put together.

I ate it all up. I couldn't imagine *not* acting. There wasn't any rejection, so I just kept going.

In 1986, I landed a one-episode role on *Valerie*, a hit TV sitcom later called *The Hogan Family* when Valerie Harper left the show. I played the next-door neighbor's niece. *Valerie* was produced by Miller Boyett Productions which, at the time, was also working with Jeff Franklin on developing a show called *Full House*. Originally *Full House* was going to be called *House of Comics* and be about three comedians living together, but they decided somewhere along the way to make it more of a family show. (Good choice!) From that one episode of *Valerie* the producers loved me enough that they decided to cast me on *Full House*. No auditions. Nothing.

I was the first person cast on the show and they wrote the character of Stephanie Tanner around me. It was amazing to fall into something so spectacular at that age. That kind of career opportunity doesn't come along every day, but I was too young at the time to realize the significance of it. Just filming anything was exciting. My family was thrilled so I knew I should be, too.

I had just turned five, a happy-go-lucky kid excited to be on the sets. We shot the pilot on the same set where they'd filmed the yellow-brick-road and poppy-field scenes for *The Wizard of Oz*. It all felt surreal.

It was shaky at first. No one thought the show was going to go anywhere. Bob Saget was the producers' top choice for the role of the dad, but he was committed to another project. Instead, John Posey played his role in the original pilot. Bob's schedule opened up soon after and we reshot with him. John Posey was out.

Even with Bob on board, expectations at ABC were low. (Hard to believe, I know.) The show barely got picked up for the first thirteen episodes. Critics hated it. They thought it was cheesy and trite and predictable, which it was—but that was '80s family sitcoms; they were all like that. (See also: *Perfect Strangers*, *Who's the Boss?*)

When the show got picked up for a full season, I didn't really understand the significance of what was happening. The older cast members were slowly realizing that this could be something special, but I was busy guessing which tooth was going to fall out next.

My parents each had a different reaction to my success.

My dad, who worked at a drywall plant in Long Beach, didn't care for the showbiz stuff. If acting took me to a cool city or offered up a fun opportunity, his instant reaction was always, "Why would I want to do that?" He was happier coming home from work, putting on *The Young Riders* (which I loved) or some other Western show, and relaxing on the couch. He was a creature of habit—waking up early every morning, reading the paper, and heading to work before the sun came up. Hollywood wasn't up his alley. But he was still a proud father. He's a man of few words, but he loved telling his friends at work about *Full House*.

My mom was thrilled about the show regardless because John Stamos was on it and in the late '80s, women loved John. (Actually even now, women love him!) I didn't know or care about *General Hospital* at that age, so to me John was just the guy whose lips were always wet and slimy when he kissed me on the forehead. There are very few things I remember clearly from the first season, but John's big, wet lips are burned on my brain. Yuck!

John's lips were big but his heart was bigger. (Insert violins/slow version of *Full House* theme song, and touching Uncle Jesse moment here.) But really, from the very beginning, we were like a family. Everyone was very warm and friendly. Bob and John didn't get along at first—who knows what they were arguing over (whose cologne smelled better?)—but pretty quickly, we all became a tight-knit group.

Of the adults, I was closest with Bob, who had three daughters in real life as well as on the show. I was a fixture among their family and was always happy spending time with them. It was nice to have real friends. Bob, though, sometimes forgot I was a little girl. One night, he decided to swing by the Laugh Factory to do a quick set. The Laugh Factory is a popular two-drink-minimum comedy club on the Sunset Strip, where adults go to get drunk and laugh at dirty jokes. It wasn't exactly the best place for a kid my age, but it was a lot of fun. I sat on the speaker and pretended to understand the jokes. "When I get home I want to make love to you badly," Bob quipped, before telling the audience his wife's response: "At least you don't overestimate yourself."

To me it was all gibberish. I laughed because everyone else was laughing, but I had no clue what he was talking about. I sat there and watched the crowd and waited for my small role: I got to flash the two-minute warning light, signaling Bob that it was time to wrap his set. It was a blast! Though the Laugh Factory would play a pivotal role in my life years later, in the late '80s it was all fun and games.

After the first season, we started picking up fans and the show got bigger and bigger. By the second season, most of the critics still couldn't stand *Full House* but it had become huge in spite of them. All of a sudden I was on a top-rated show and people began to recognize me. It was all very strange, but my parents helped me cope with the changing environment and kept me grounded.

I still had to make my bed every morning, help with the

dishes, and do chores around the house. I was, for all intents and purposes, a regular kid with rules and bedtimes and homework to be checked. Other than the TV gig, life was normal. My parents made sure of that. They stressed to me that *Full House* was just what I did and how I made money, but that if I ever hated it or felt too much pressure, I could stop at any time.

At six, I didn't think quitting was a viable option. I loved acting and performing and had no plans to ever stop.

chapter three

STUCK IN THE MIDDLE

i didn't watch *Full House* while I was doing the show. I didn't need to. I lived it, and sometimes it was hard to tell the difference between Stephanie Tanner's life and my own. I wasn't really a middle child begging for attention and struggling to figure out where I belonged, but when the cameras stopped rolling, I still felt Stephanie's pain.

On set, I just wanted to be a kid. I was six. That wasn't too much to ask was it? But *Full House* was a job and I was expected to behave like a miniature adult. When I first started, I'd get in trouble for playing hide-and-seek on the set. Directors would be ready to shoot a scene and I would be hiding under Stephanie's bed. It didn't go over well.

I also threw an occasional temper tantrum. On an episode called "Middle Age Crazy," no one pays attention to Stephanie so she marries her friend Harry Takayama. In a dream sequence, she goes off to Mars and no one cares. (That happens to every kid, right?)

For that dream scene I went to what was then MGM studios to have two costumes made. There, I saw the dress that Dorothy wore in *The Wizard of Oz,* and it was a big deal to me, even then, to have a dress made by the same studio that had made Dorothy's. My dress was gorgeous: blue with feathers on the bottom and rhinestones and all the stuff that little girls love. I remember floating around the stage in that dress, twirling with my boa. I was in hog heaven. When it came time to put on the other outfit—a pants outfit—I was horrified. I started crying and refused to change. I was sitting on the steps of the entryway to the Tanner living room set, bawling uncontrollably because life was so unfair.

Regular kids get to throw temper tantrums once in a while and it's no big deal. If a kid wants to wear her Halloween costume to school in the middle of December, it's fine. Go for it. But I had to take off the dress. You don't screw around on the set of a hit TV show. It was those little things that made me realize I didn't have the luxury to just be a kid. You can't hide under your bed or refuse to take off your favorite outfit. I couldn't even get sick.

If I had a cold, the producers called the set doctor who gave me medicine and I got to work. One time I had the flu and they were forced to stop production of the show for a week. I was extremely sick. It was before they did the "A Pox in Our House" episode, which is still one of my favorites. Stephanie gets the chicken pox and tries to sneak out of the house in a little trench coat. I love that!

I was panicking because I could see how stressed-out my mom was after the producers called her saying, "Can she come to work? She can come to work, right?" I was throwing up and had a fever. My mom was torn, trying not to piss off the producers (it's a huge deal to stop production for a week) and at the same time, still trying to be a mom.

She was always stuck in the middle. Even when I freaked out over that dress, my mom had the dual role of manager, with the attitude "Tough shit, kid, you've got to change the outfit" and mom, who knew her little girl just wanted to wear a dress. The whole process was tough for us both.

Don't get me wrong, our producers were caring and loved us like family. We were very fortunate to work in an environment like that. But I always knew in the back of my mind, even as a kid, that my needs came second to the big picture. There was very little time for me to be a kid back then, which is what I really wanted.

It wasn't any better for me at school. I was smarter than your average six-year-old, which had helped me land *Full House* in the first place. I skipped kindergarten and was already reading at a fifth- or sixth-grade level. Teachers wanted to skip me to second grade but my mom put a stop to that, knowing that I'd be completely out of place.

By the show's second season (even though critics still thought the show was pretty lame) *Full House* was a hit with children and their parents. The kids in my second-grade class at Fairmont Elementary School in Southern California recognized me from television, but at that age being on the show didn't make me very popular.

I didn't think being on television was that big a deal. To me, some kids played soccer or took karate. I went to work and filmed a television show. It didn't seem any different from other after-school activities, but my classmates obviously didn't see it that way.

Making friends was hard enough being the youngest in the class, and it didn't help that I would leave school in the afternoon to rehearse or film an episode three weeks out of every month. Every time I started to make a friend or two, I would have to leave and go to work. I often missed out on lunch and other key times when kids actually became friends. Plus, spending my afternoons working in an adult environment made it difficult for me to understand what it meant to be a kid. When everyone else went to the playground, I worked my way over to the library. I felt more comfortable hanging out with the school librarian than I did with the kids who were closer to my own age.

Kids started whispering behind my back, saying, "There's the girl from *Full House*. That's her. That's Stephanie Tanner." I just couldn't take it—all I wanted was for people to see that that character wasn't me, that I wasn't Stephanie Tanner, that she was just who I was on TV. Why didn't they understand that?

My mom would console me, telling me they were just jealous, or using her always-popular phrase, "If they are making fun of you, at least you know they are watching the show." But that didn't make it any easier.

The whole concept was too hard for me to grasp. The other kids would be playing on the seesaw and running around playing tag and I'm saying "How rude!" in front of a three-hundred-person live studio audience. There were camera crews, directors, and producers expecting things from me every day and I remember looking around at school thinking, "You guys don't do that, too?"

They didn't, and they reminded me of that pretty often. Later, I realized that kids make fun of one another for pretty much anything. It doesn't matter what it is; kids will find anything. For me, it was being on *Full House*.

I took it personally. I thought something was wrong with me and all I wanted was to blend in as much as possible, to be like everyone else. I hated being different and being picked on. People quoted me in class saying "How rude!" or something else they had heard in an episode. Other favorites were, "What would Danny Tanner do?" or "Where's Uncle Jesse now?" Eventually it was too much for me to take. One day, I completely lost it.

I was minding my own business (probably being precocious as usual, raising my hand to answer every question the teacher asked) and a girl in class started making fun of me. I can't remember what she said, but she was pointing and everyone was laughing.

I kept telling her to shut up and I was getting angrier and angrier. She wouldn't stop. Why wouldn't she stop?

Everyone kept laughing. I couldn't take it. I stood up,

turned around, picked up my blue plastic chair, and chucked it across the table at her.

As Stephanie Tanner would say . . . "Pin a rose on your nose" . . . bitch!

The kids were shocked and I felt like a big idiot. What had I just done? My teacher was not particularly happy with me (although she never seemed particularly happy about anything). Of course, I had to go sit in the principal's office.

But I got away with it. They didn't even call my mom. I remember going home and, for three days, I was terrified every time the phone rang. But nothing ever happened. My teacher never said anything about it, and I was in the clear. That was my first angry outburst, and throughout my elementary school years, I had many more. I didn't know how to deal with other people picking on me and making me feel different. I would reach a point and lash out. I was kicked out of handball games and tetherball, and no one wanted to play with me.

On the *Full House* set, I also struggled to find my place. As an only child in real life, I enjoyed my own space and my own things, but playing a middle child on the show turned me into the middle kid on set with my pseudoextended family. Ashley and Mary-Kate Olsen were the cute little infants and got a lot of the attention. Candace Cameron was eleven years old and getting to the age where she was too cool to talk to me.

I looked up to Candace. In the beginning, she would go to school in the mornings as I did, so we had that in common. Eventually, Candace had so many problems in middle school and high school—kids were mean and even violent toward her—that she said screw it, and left for private tutoring. The Olsens were also tutored on set. Even something that seemed so inconsequential—attending regular school—set me apart from my castmates. I was the only one who needed to have my foot in both worlds; I was alone in wanting to hold on to that little bit of normalcy, no matter how painful or difficult it was.

For a couple of years, Candace and I didn't get along at all. It was the typical stuff you might go through as sisters. She didn't want to hang out with me because I was so young; clearly she didn't get the memo that I was reading at a fifth-grade level! I'd try to get her attention saying, "Pay attention to me! Look, I have a funny knock-knock joke," but she'd just walk away. (Where was Harry Takayama when I needed him?)

One time Candace hurt my feelings so badly that I decided to write something mean about her on the back wall of the living-room set. I don't remember exactly what it said but I'm pretty sure the F-word was involved—and I doubt I even knew what it meant. But there it was in big black Sharpie. The home audience couldn't see it, but Candace could and that was all that mattered.

Like any kid, I tried to deny that I had done it, but there wasn't exactly anyone else I could blame for my graffiti. The Olsens weren't even writing yet.

Candace was a tough audience, but I liked taking care of Mary-Kate and Ashley. They were too little to run away when I wanted to tell a bad joke.

By the beginning of the third season, I was going through a middle-child complex. I loved acting and being on the set, but I didn't have anyone around me that was my age; I loved school and learning, but no one there liked me. Just like a middle child, I didn't know where I fit in. It was the beginning of a bad cycle—wanting to be like other people, feeling like there was something missing in me, lashing out and making it worse. It's only now that I see how the seeds of my addiction were there even before I ever picked up a drink or a drug. My feelings of inadequacy, which eventually led to the need to drink and do drugs, started early. I was full of self-esteem issues. I felt alone, and it seemed like there was no way out.

The thing with being a normal kid is that most kids usually quit soccer or karate eventually. My parents always told me that if at any point I wanted to leave the show, I could. But we were three seasons in and I knew the producers weren't just going to replace me. When characters had been replaced on other shows, it was obvious and never really worked. I knew I had to stick with it, and to be honest, quitting never crossed my mind. I knew only that I wanted to be normal and, at a young age, realized that was never going to happen.

chapter four

WHEN YOU WISH YOU WERE A STAR

the idea of normalcy went completely out the window when the show hit its stride in the third and fourth seasons. Luckily, my parents still kept me grounded. "This will come to an end someday," my mom would say. "Sure thing, crazy lady," was usually the response that went through my mind, but never came out of my mouth.

Regardless of what I was doing during the week for *Full House*, my parents always tried to give me a regular childhood away from the set. Every Friday, my dad would come to the taping, then take my mom and me to Ed Debevic's, a once-popular restaurant, to celebrate the week's end. Nine times out of ten I'd be asleep on my dad's lap before the food came, but he enjoyed the family time so I didn't want to disappoint him. On the weekends, I went rollerblading and bike riding around the neighborhood with the private-school kids who lived across the street and every now and then I was just another kid.

To make life more enjoyable, my mom would surprise me with fun trips. If there was a change of clothes sitting on the passenger's seat of the car when she picked me up from school, I knew I was going to Disneyland. She always made the effort to put together great mother-daughter days. She even took me to Williamsburg for the release of the American Girl Felicity doll—a colonial era doll that I was really into. We spent a week out there together enjoying the American Girl tea party and going backstage at the play the company put on.

But, as the show got bigger, my time off got shorter. Summers became less about family time at Big Bear and more about promotional appearances, charity events, and screaming kids at malls.

I guess the first time the whole celebrity aspect of my job hit me was during a mall appearance in Des Moines, Iowa. My mom's side of the family lived in Iowa and my cousins were able to come see me host an autograph signing at a store opening. We were all excited. What neither they nor I expected, though, was the huge crowd that showed up.

When we arrived, the event organizers told me that instead of the fifteen hundred or so people they'd expected, around six thousand people had come out. It was mayhem! There wasn't room for anyone.

They set me up to sign autographs for a couple of hours but after twenty minutes it was total chaos. People were pushing and shoving and they had to take me to the back of the store. The cops and the fire marshall arrived and shut things down. To get me out of there in one piece, they dressed me up like a boy with a hat and big jacket, and escorted me out of the mall into the back of a cop car. As the limo I'd arrived in drove off without me, people trailed it, thinking I was inside. I rendezvoused with the limo three miles away when the coast was clear.

That night, the local news ran a story about my appearance. They showed kids crying and interviewed people who were upset that I had canceled. I sat there, watching parents say, "I can't believe she would abandon her fans like that." I was not only frustrated that I had disappointed people, but also completely overwhelmed that something I'd been involved in was on the news.

It was then that I realized that *Full House* was a big deal. Of course, I thought the show was really cool, but I didn't quite get it—how many people were actually watching this show. Families watched this show together, *every* Friday? Really? Watching that moment at the mall on the evening news I began to understand that *Full House* was much bigger than I was. It was a little scary.

There were some perks to the success though. With the show doing so well, we had newfound funding that allowed us to do some great episodes. We took off to shoot in Hawaii, which turned into a bit of a disaster. The storyline was that the Tanner family gets lost on a boat tour. Knowing we would be spending a good amount of time at sea, producers, afraid we would get seasick, gave us Dramamine. It knocked us all out. We didn't have any lines, but in the scene I'm asleep sitting up in the corner of the boat and the working Olsen twin is asleep standing up, leaning against the table.

Later during the week, Dave Coulier broke his toe walking into the edge of his bed and Jeff Franklin, the show's executive producer, snapped his Achilles tendon playing tennis. There were problems all around!

But we had fun in Hawaii, too. We had a big luau and swam with the dolphins. Candace was super scared of the dolphins. Every time she had to even touch one she would squeal like, well, a dolphin.

By this trip, Andrea Barber and I were very close. I was tutored on set Thursday and Friday, and we had the same studio teacher (unlike Candace) so we were together a lot. She helped me with my homework and always made me laugh. Plus she put in the effort to relate to me by talking about my feelings and asking about my real interests.

One day in Hawaii, Andrea and I went to the botanical gardens. On the way out we saw a dead frog completely flattened on the ground. It was in a weird position and looked like it had died doing the tango. Andrea and I named it Slim and would pose in the same position, with one arm out to the side and the other on the body. It was a running joke throughout the trip. RIP, Slim. We hardly knew ye.

Producers also managed to get the OK for a Las Vegas trip. In the episode, Joey is opening for Wayne Newton and we filmed at the arena in the Las Vegas Hilton. After work we all took a private tour of the Elvis suite—a cool room on the thirtieth floor of the Hilton, which was known as the International Hotel during Elvis's time. It still had bullet holes

in the wall from when Elvis would go crazy and shoot his
gun off. I was in my own world and after the tour, when I got
in the elevator, I realized that I had left my mom behind. I
had the wherewithal to find a producer who ultimately re-
united us. She ran down the hallway screaming when she finally saw me. The twenty minutes we were apart probably
shaved a couple of years off her life, she was so nervous. It
was just one of the many times I would drive my mom
insane. The truth is, had I been tall enough to reach the
blackjack table, she'd probably still be looking for me to this
day.

We also performed with the Beach Boys and when they
came on the show in the episode "Beach Boy Bingo," my
mom was in heaven. She and I would bond on our car rides
to school and to work listening to them and while I also
knew all the words to Digital Underground's "The Humpty
Dance" (I didn't have a clue what they meant but, needless
to say, my mom didn't like it) she and I connected with
oldies music. That was our go-to music whenever we were
together.

Having the Beach Boys on set was amazing and the singing and dancing was a blast. We never knew what we were
going to get from Brian Wilson, who always seemed to be
playing with half a deck. Once, when the studio teacher fed
the Olsen du jour her line—that's how they got their scenes
done when they were young—Brian repeated it as if they
were feeding the line to him. Everyone started laughing. I
think producers should have made "You got it, dude" a Beach
Boys catch phrase!

With Vegas and Hawaii and all the fun, the show took over my life. It also started coming first during the school year and I started missing important school activities.

One of the huge traumas of my elementary school life was missing outdoors camp. Everybody else got to go up to the mountains for the week, learn about leaves and pinecones, play outside, and be in the big yearbook spread documenting the trip. I didn't get to do any of that.

Of course, the reason I didn't get to outdoors camp is we were shooting in Walt Disney World for two weeks. Not so bad, I know, but I threw a fit. I felt left out.

Disney had its obvious thrills. We didn't wait on line for any of the rides and went backstage, rode in the parade, and ate at great restaurants. We got treated like stars and it was the best feeling in the world for a little girl.

But it wasn't all fun and games. During filming, tons of people were standing around snapping candid photos. I hated it. I might have been scratching my nose and people would snap away. I felt like a circus animal. I was still a little kid and it freaked me out.

One morning during all the hoopla, I didn't feel well. My mom walked me over to a public restroom and we went into the stall. While I was, uh, getting rid of my stomachache, a teenage girl came in and walked over to the stall where I was sitting with my pants around my ankles. She reached under the stall and asked me to sign an autograph for her.

My mom was furious!

"Get out of here," she yelled. "How dare you! Are you brainless? How could you do that?"

I realized that I was not going to have my own space, anywhere—at least not while the show was filming. I needed to be on, happy, and ready to sign someone's sheet of paper underneath the bathroom stall.

A few days later at the happiest place on Earth, we were taping at Disney's MGM Studios. The crew was trying to clear the crowd out so we could come in and tape a scene. The stage managers seated us in a small section of the stands and asked us not to sign any autographs as they cleared people out, as it would slow the crowd down. As I sat there with my mom I noticed an older lady, probably in her fifties, creeping toward the stands. She walked up the stairs, leaned over a little bit, and asked for an autograph.

"I'm sorry," I said politely. "I can't."

My mom/manager/bodyguard who was the only one running interference jumped in. "They told her that right now she can't sign any autographs," she said nicely. It wasn't good enough.

This lady flipped out. "You are such a selfish little bitch! Your mother's a bitch!" She screamed at me and called me every name in the book. I burst into tears. It felt like I couldn't win. I couldn't keep everyone happy.

But whenever I did public appearances, I'd try to be nice to everybody and sign autographs for as long as possible, sometimes for four hours straight. But then an event manager would start closing it down, and there would still be hundreds of people in line. I wanted to get to all the fans who had taken the time to come see me, and would feel terrible that I couldn't and drained from trying to keep everyone happy.

Really, I was just too young to understand that it was OK to have my own limits and boundaries. My mom had my back every step of the way, but I still had trouble saying no to people.

Putting the few bad moments aside, I was fully prepared to return to school and wow all my classmates with stories of Minnie and Mickey Mouse. Why? Because they'll like me (as Walt Disney would say). Trying to share these cool experiences, I walked back into class and talked about how we got to go on this parade, and got to go here and there. It didn't go over so well. All the other kids acted as if they hated me.

My mom stepped in. "Maybe you shouldn't tell people all the cool things you get to do because they might not like you for it," she said.

I didn't get it.

My mom would say they were jealous of me, but I was jealous of them. I thought it would be cool to be able to just go to school all day. I envied the normalcy of their lives. I didn't understand why they would want mine, which was getting even more overwhelming.

Just going to school had become difficult. Never mind that I couldn't be involved with school plays because I never had the time to rehearse or that I was labeled a weirdo because I had to work when other kids were busy playing. The bigger concern was stalkers.

People would call my mom and ask her if she knew where I was at that moment, even though I'd be just down the hall. People threatened to abduct me, take me out of the country, and marry me. It was terrifying. I met with Gavin de Becker, the big security guy, who made sure I was OK. He sat my family down, told all of us the concerns, and explained what we needed to do so I stayed safe. There were a lot of limitations and going anywhere in public was always a procedure. I couldn't even walk to school. In the end, the happiest place on Earth was actually the three walls that made up that enormous how-does-Danny-Tanner-afford-that-house we called home.

chapter five

KISS AND TELL

the show was in full stride from 1991 to 1993 when it was ranked in the Nielsen top ten. TGIF and *Full House* were household names, everyone on the show was a star, and almost everyone had his or her own star moments.

In our on-set bedroom we, like many kids in the early '90s, had posters of people like Paula Abdul and George Michael on our walls. During the height of the show, John Stamos *had* Paula Abdul. She came to the set every once in a while, armed with extra security. No one on the set treated her differently, but there was an air of celebrity around her. She was pretty normal back then, before Simon Cowell entered her life.

Once, John got us tickets to see her in concert. I was really excited about it, but I got sick at the last minute and couldn't go. A few days later, she sent me a signed program

that said, "Keep dancing. Wish you were here. Love, Paula."
For a little girl who loved to dance, I was ecstatic to get that
letter.

John also brought George Michael into our lives. One
night Candace, my mom, and I went with John to George
Michael's Cover to Cover Los Angeles concert. George Michael shaking his ass while singing "Faith"—even as a preteen I could appreciate that. John got us all backstage and
Candace and John immediately ran up to grab photos of and
autographs from George Michael. But I couldn't do it. I was
too nervous to ask!

John was the cool uncle, even in real life, playing
music and bringing his famous friends around. He always
hosted the beginning-of-the-season barbecue at his *Miami
Vice*–style dream house off Mulholland Drive. It was all
white and turquoise and leathery—a Don Johnson wet
dream.

Dave Coulier was pretty cool in his own right. He used
to rollerblade around the set with his hockey stick and little
orange ball. He dated Alanis Morissette, who was always
friendly when she came to the studio and who seemed like
such a nice girl. The most famous thing to come out of that
relationship? Her hit song "You Oughta Know," which angrily
detailed "the mess [Dave] left when [he] went away." While
it became an anthem for every dumped girl in America, I
could never light a candle and listen to "You Oughta Know"
while cutting up photos of an ex, because any song about
Dave Coulier just makes me giggle.

Dave was also responsible for one of the on-set *Full*

House hook ups we had during the show's run. (He's a stud, I know.) In an episode called "Those Better Not Be the Days," the guys are being bossed around by the girls (typical!) and fantasize about how the future would look if they grew old while D.J., Stephanie, and Michelle continued to call the shots. Playing the role of "adult Michelle" was an actor by the name of Jayne Modean, a very attractive former model. With the help of a few Bullwinkle impressions, no doubt, Dave charmed the pants off her. They dated and married soon after and had a son together before divorcing a couple years later.

John dated Chelsea Noble who was in a couple of episodes during his mullet years. It didn't last very long. She ultimately married Candace's brother, Kirk Cameron, who starred on *Growing Pains* and spent his youth on the cover of every teen magazine imaginable.

Besides John and Dave, everyone kept a low profile. Bob Saget was a married man during the *Full House* years, so he was more of a family guy. Candace, like her brother, was growing into a more Christian-centric lifestyle and wasn't exactly one to land in the gossip pages. Mary-Kate and Ashley were only six years old in 1992, but they were already creating their monster empire. They were worked overtime back then, creating hit TV movies *To Grandmother's House We Go* and *Double, Double, Toil and Trouble*. They were at the perfect level of cuteness during the height of the show, which really launched their careers.

I, on the other hand—I went through an awkward stage

that is forever documented in syndication and on DVD. The timing was terrible. During the biggest years of the show, I was no longer the sweet kid with the witty one-liners. All of a sudden I was a preteen lost in between the Olsens' awww-inducing cuteness and Candace's maturity. My teeth were everywhere! I developed a lisp and had to go to speech therapy after school. Saying Stephanie is cute only for so long and then you have to fix it.

There were so many embarrassing moments that I had to go through on camera. I remember one incident where it was one of the Olsen girls and I on set. (I've forgotten which one, they looked a lot alike!) We were doing a scene in front of the whole studio audience and it was during the years when my teeth were coming in. I had one tooth that wouldn't come down; it was just sticking out of my gums. About thirty seconds before we were about to start filming, the Olsen twin turns to me and says, "Why do you have a tooth growing out of there?" I turned bright red and almost started to cry. Everyone was laughing, thinking how cute she was for saying that, because, you know, "kids say the darndest things." I, however, was mortified.

Ashley and Mary-Kate were always fascinated with my teeth. When they were losing their first teeth, I had one or two still hanging on for dear life. So when I would be ready to lose one, they had to be there to watch me pull it out. It was silly but they loved to watch me wiggle a loose tooth.

While most kids had bad teeth and braces and atrocious '80s outfits alongside only their friends, I had the whole world watching. I started becoming much more conscious of how other people were viewing me. I would constantly think, "I'm going to have to say this line and everybody at school is going to hear it and think I'm so stupid" or, "I'm so not cool because I'm wearing this outfit." *Full House* was sort of cheesy and over the top and I was *that* girl.

I became very aware that I was just the middle kid that wasn't the cute one or the older one. I wasn't quite sure who I was—either in character or in real life. The lines were often blurred. Although I had a good head on my shoulders and knew it was just television, everybody else saw me as Stephanie Tanner. Separating real life from fiction was difficult because I really did have teeth like that and I really was awkward. And, more and more, my important childhood milestones were lived out on camera as Stephanie's moments—not mine. I was always wishing for a kissing scene like Candace, and of course, when I finally got one I wanted to take back that wish.

During the fourth season, Stephanie uses her charm and aggressive preteen lust to plant a kiss on Rusty when the clock strikes midnight in an episode called "Happy New Year." Sounds easy enough—except it was my first time *ever* kissing a boy. I thought people were going to make fun of me or think that we were really boyfriend and girlfriend or, or, or, or . . . I thought up horror story after horror story until my brain was about to explode. To make matters worse, my mom was on set. I asked her to leave when we rehearsed the scene because it was too embarrassing for me. We rehearsed for a couple of days but we didn't actually do the kiss until tape day. In the end, it was like pecking my grandmother.

Eventually I/Stephanie got the hang of it. Future episodes had me kissing guys on opposing baseball teams and locking lips at parties. I came a long way in a short time!

The real world was a bit tougher. Boys were a complete enigma to me. I had no idea what to do with them. I didn't have my first real kiss until middle school, which was later than most people I knew. His name was Victor and he was in my seventh-period art class. He had slicked-back hair, big, baggy shorts, and a tough-guy attitude. He also had these amazing blue eyes, which won me over instantly. One day after school we were hanging out behind the art building and I just kissed him. It was only a second or two but it felt like an eternity. What was I supposed to do with my tongue? There was no tongue on *Full House*. I felt like I had no idea what I was doing.

"My mom is waiting," I told him before I ran off. I was terrified. He stayed my boyfriend for a few weeks and then he moved on, probably to a better kisser.

Somehow it all seemed harder without the studio audience. At school, I packed in all my classes before noon and then I was gone. I remember looking around and thinking, "Am I missing something? How do they all seem to know how to be friends?" Everyone knew how to be social. It felt like they must have taught a class on it that I missed. It was probably taught in the afternoons.

I started to give up at school and with kids my age altogether. Instead, I became friendly with people on the set.
Ultimately, it felt like I had a lot of aunts and uncles. That
didn't help when you were in a stage where you wanted to
practice your kissing.

chapter six

THE LAST "HOW RUDE!"

the one thing I could always count on—no matter how rough things were going at school or how awkward I felt on set or how lost I felt in this world—was that every Tuesday through Friday I had a place to go, lines to read, and an important role to play. Ever since I was five years old, I'd been working on *Full House*. The gig might have changed as I aged, but the cast was like family and the set was familiar and comforting.

Even during hiatus we couldn't get enough of one another. One summer, just after we wrapped, the cast of *Full House* got tickets to Janet Jackson's tour concert in Los Angeles. My mom wasn't happy about letting me go, but I was a huge Janet fan so she wasn't going to deny me the thrill of seeing her live.

We all went together in a limo, stopping first at Ed

Debevic's in West Hollywood for dinner. After we ate, the kids went out to the limo while the adults paid the bill. Inside the car, I leaned over to tie my shoe and BAM!, an explosion scared the bejesus out of all of us. The window of the limo exploded. I screamed and ran out of the car, yelling at the top of my lungs down La Cienega Boulevard.

We had been shot at. I don't know if it was with a pellet gun or a real gun, but I was freaking out. One of the adults called the cops and filled out a report before we all hopped into two station wagons to get to the concert, which, by the way, was amazing.

After the show, Bob decided he should tell my mom what happened. "OK, Janice, don't freak out," he told her. "Jodie's OK." He explained the story as she grabbed me and hugged me tight. She was a nervous wreck. Since no one was hurt, I thought it was pretty cool. I got shot at. It was instant street cred.

The relationship I developed with the cast over the show's eight-year run was a strong, deep bond. Lori Loughlin even picked up the motherly role for us when we needed it. If the kids were working too hard or if any of us looked like we weren't feeling well, she was the first to make sure we were taken care of or felt better. Even when filming the episode where D.J. becomes anorexic for thirty minutes, Lori made sure the kids knew that it was a storyline for the character and not Candace in real life.

Our producers were always coming up with excuses to put big-boobed, hot women into our family show, and the gym scene in that episode was packed with models, in spandex no less. As a joke (and probably to make sure we girls didn't start to become self-conscious about our bodies) Lori corralled Candace, the Olsen du jour, and me to stuff our shirts with huge balls of tissues. We all came walking out on set—little girls and Lori—with giant boobs. Jeff Franklin fell out of his chair laughing. It was a great example of what kind of person Lori was with us.

Andrea Barber, too, was like a sister to me and a daughter to the other adults. She's nothing like her Kimmy Gibbler character; she's intelligent and mellow. During the eighth season, Andrea had to work the night of her senior prom. No girl wants to miss out on that opportunity, so the producers worked it out and she shot all of her scenes early in the evening. The hair and makeup people on set got her prom ready and her date came to the studio to pick her up. He had the corsage and the whole deal. It must have been a terrifying experience for him, but he hung in there as the whole cast (still in wardrobe) took photos and sent Andrea off to prom like a real family would have.

Those kinds of close relationships don't develop on sets very often. We all knew we were in a unique situation. Birthdays and Christmases were always a big deal on set, and the producers as well as the adult cast members did their best to make us all feel like regular kids. For my thirteenth birthday, I had a huge party at Disneyland. The whole cast came and Bob Saget and Dave Coulier gave sweet and funny speeches about how much I meant to them and about how proud they were of me. Bob called it my Bat Mitzvah. He was friendly with Paul Pressler, the president of Disneyland, and they arranged to have the Disneyland marching band come and play "Happy Birthday."

My birthday always fell during our working season and I loved it! The crew would bring out a big birthday cake and balloons and everyone would sing. We did that for everyone. Holidays were equally exciting. Jeff Franklin gave me a bike one Christmas and I got to ride it around the set. "If this show is still going when she's sixteen," he told my mom, "I'll buy her a car." Unfortunately, that day didn't come.

I knew *Full House* had to end at some point—my parents reminded me of that nearly every day. I was young but I understood that. Even when we were just on hiatus, I knew that my on-set family would be off doing their own things in the summers and that at the end of the day, they all went home to their own lives, with their real families.

In the eighth season, the good-bye was for good and sadly we didn't get much warning. When we started that season there was some talk that it might be the last, but it was never official so I didn't think much about it. About five weeks before the last show, we were told that ABC wasn't going to pick the show up for an additional season. There was talk that we were going with the new WB Television Network, so everyone was filled with a sense of uncertainty.

With just two weeks left, we were told that the show was simply too expensive for The WB and that *Full House* would be ending. That moment of "this is it," which my parents had always tried to prepare me for, had suddenly arrived. The life I had known for eight years was over.

The last week was hard for everyone. The last episode

we filmed (which was not the last one to air) was a Stephanie-filled episode, and the last scene we filmed was just Bob and I. In that scene, Stephanie is walking out the front door and runs back in and gives him a big hug and says, "Thanks for being a great dad." For viewers it was typical *Full House* sappiness, but for me, that moment was tough. I tried so hard not to cry. I knew once we finished that scene, the show was over. It was the last time I would walk through that door. Ironically, in the very first episode, the show started with Stephanie not wanting to say good-bye to Grandma through the front door. Everything had come full circle at that moment and it hit me like a ton of bricks—this is really it.

During the last curtain, everyone was standing backstage crying. I felt like I was losing my family—everyone that I had been around every day for eight years. The way I had lived my whole life was changing and instead of realizing it was just a job coming to an end, at thirteen I felt as if my life was ending.

In the weeks that followed, the sadness turned to confusion. I had no idea what to do. Did I want to keep acting? Maybe. I was also about to start high school, young for my age since I'd skipped a grade. I thought that had potential to work out nicely, since I could jump right in and be a normal high school kid. But, I'd been working for so long that I couldn't stop thinking like a mini adult. What about work? Was I now a has-been? Was my career over?

I couldn't let it end like that, so I attempted to hit the audition circuit. Other than *Full House*, I didn't have much else on my résumé: a few commercials and a cameo on *The Mickey Mouse Club* with Justin Timberlake, Britney Spears, Christina Aguilera, and Ryan Gosling. Sadly, none of them ever made anything of themselves. It's really tragic, because they were so talented.

Working on set with them was a wild experience. I was the star making the cameo so I got a lot of attention, and I'd be lying if I said I didn't enjoy every bit of it—especially from Ryan. I had the biggest crush on him. After the show we called each other a few times. My heart would race every time I dialed. One time I called him and he was at Justin Timberlake's house. Instead of paying attention to me he was focused on goofing off with Justin, each of them daring the other to run around the house in just his underwear. Typical boy stuff. I didn't understand boys at all and needless to say, that relationship was over before it started.

As fun as the *MMC* experience was, it didn't help me land another acting job. I was officially labeled Stephanie Tanner. Sometimes I wouldn't even get auditions because casting directors would tell my agent, "She's just the girl from *Full House*. We know what she can do." There was no chance to do anything different.

Everyone was in the same boat. John Stamos must have seen this coming because he tried to change his image even before *Full House* ended—playing a kidnapping rapist in an ABC TV movie called *Captive*. It was as far away from Uncle Jesse as he could possibly go. Clearly, for any of us who wanted to work again, it was an uphill battle.

For me it was especially challenging since I started so

young and was seemingly forever burned into people's brains as Stephanie Judith Tanner. At one audition, the casting director took one look at me and started to gush. "Oh my God, you're Stephanie. I love your show. Can you say 'How rude!' for me?" Inside, my blood was boiling as I cleared my throat and delivered the line in perfect falsetto. It was devastating. I was there auditioning for an important role and all this woman cared about was *Full House*?

"How rude!"

Before I knew it we were talking about John Stamos's hair (no I didn't really cut it in that episode) and everything about the show you could imagine. I was up for a dramatic role and thinking how odd it was that the director would do this before a serious scene. I started wondering why I was even there. After the audition, she told me I was great and that she loved my show. I didn't get the part.

That audition shook me up. After that, I'd walk into auditions and spend the whole time thinking about how much I sucked. I lost all my self-confidence. When I was younger I could walk into a room and just own it, but now, as a teenager, I wanted to blend into a wall and be like everybody else.

I tried acting classes, but that didn't help much. I did well and the teachers always loved me, but the fact that I couldn't land roles started to frustrate them, too. Their student wasn't getting the right opportunities and it was making everyone look bad.

My parents were really supportive and tried to help me through it all but I don't think they knew what to do either.

There is no manual for parenting and certainly no instruc-
tions for dealing with your thirteen-year-old daughter when
she's lost her job after eight years—you can't look that up in
a book! My mom tried to support me as much as possible,
but the failure was taking its toll on us both.

Once, I went in for an audition and there was a line of
girls, some I knew by now, who all sort of looked like me. We
were all in the same boat, trying to get this one job. I had already had the success that these girls wanted to just taste, so
I didn't have the hunger for it that they did. I went in and
read the lines without any energy or enthusiasm because I
just didn't care.

My mom saw that and was not happy. "Do you want to
do this or not?" she asked. "It's fine if you don't but we have
to stop wasting our time pretending."

I simply didn't know what I wanted. One day I would
want to be in a movie and the next day I would want to go to
my fourth- and fifth-period classes and have Spanish homework. I had always had the distraction of *Full House* to keep
my mind busy, but with that gone I was completely confused
and at a loss for what I was going to do next, where I was
going to be, and more important, who I was.

My mom, my agent, and I sat down and talked about
how we could rework my image—get different head shots
done, maybe go under a different name so that when people
saw my head shots they wouldn't automatically think, "Oh,
Jodie Sweetin from *Full House*." It seems silly now, but that
was the plan. It was like a midlife crisis, but instead of getting an earring and buying a Corvette, I was taking sexy

photos and changing my name. We were willing to try anything; my parents just wanted me to be happy.

I was lost. Thirteen years old without a job. What's a girl to do? At that point, it seemed like a good idea to do what most every other girl in the world was doing, so I loaded up my Trapper Keeper and went to high school.

chapter seven

CREATURE OF HABIT

i was still only thirteen years old when I started the ninth grade because I had skipped kindergarten. I was fresh off *Full House*, filled with spunk, and ready to finally be a regular kid.

I enrolled at the Orange County High School of the Arts, which was a school within my local high school, Los Alamitos High School.

I was there to focus on the arts classes—drama, dance, and all that good stuff—but first and foremost, I wanted to make some friends.

They had a big freshman welcome dance hosted by the student council to help people like me achieve just that. The school officials took the parents to the auditorium for a speech about what to expect, while the kids partied in the gym. They warned the parents about how their children would change and mature and about how the girls, especially, should look out for the older boys.

I, of course, immediately gravitated to the older boys inside the party. In fact, while that speech was going on, I was in the gym making out with the student body president. He came up to me, we started dancing, and just like that on the first day, I was the girl who was making out at the welcoming party.

Afterward I found out that not only did he have a girlfriend, but also the whole thing had been just a dare. His friends bet him that he couldn't make out with the girl from *Full House*. He won.

It was a bad first impression and an awkward start to high school. His girlfriend would stare me down in the hallways and rumors about me started to swirl.

As the first year went by, I tried connecting with the kids in the arts program. Unfortunately, those classes took place from 1:00 p.m. to 5:30 p.m., the time I had to miss if I went on auditions. Although I still had the acting bug, when an audition would come up, I was more and more likely to opt for the movies, hang out with a friend, and just be a part of school whenever possible.

That didn't always fly with my mom.

"Don't you get that all of these kids are in this school to do what you have the opportunity to be doing right now?" my mom would say when I would bitch about leaving. "They're all here hoping to go audition and learn how to do this. They all want to be actors. You *are* an actor. You can go and audition for a real job."

Good point, Mom.

Complaining about leaving for auditions didn't win over any friends. My mom was right. (I hate it when that happens!) My classmates were trying to achieve what I had already done, and none of them sympathized with my problems balancing school and work.

High school is hard enough as it is. Kids make fun of one another as they walk the halls, sometimes for no reason at all, and I was that girl from TV. The jokes pretty much wrote themselves. I was always uncomfortable; no matter where I went on campus, people would say, "Oh, there's the girl from *Full House*." There were rumors about me even before I got to the high school. People said I was a brat and that I thought I was better than everybody. What they didn't know was that I would have gladly traded places with any of them. They all seemed so perfect.

The people I gravitated toward were the cheerleaders and popular kids, but I always felt on the outside of the group. I was with them, but I was different. To blend in, I decided to try out for song leading, which fell between cheerleading and dance squad on the extracurricular activity hierarchy. I took some private dance lessons in preparation for tryouts and worked really hard. On the second day of tryouts, I looked around and decided I didn't like these girls enough to spend this much or any more time with them. I also feared I wasn't going to be good enough. So, I packed my bags and walked out in the middle of the tryout. It wasn't for me. I decided to just accept the fact that I was the outsider.

Most of the time I felt out of place. I was always worried that I would have nothing interesting to say or wouldn't be able to relate to the other kids. My biggest fear was that someone would strike up a conversation and I wouldn't be able to come up with funny responses. As far back as I can remember, I believed that the "real me" wasn't interesting enough. The persona of Stephanie Tanner and the girl who plays Stephanie Tanner were interesting, but just being me without her? That's scary.

With my low self-esteem and confusion over who I really was, I put on a pretty dress and hauled my then fourteen-year-old, unemployed ass to Woodland Hills Country Club in the Valley for Candace Cameron's wedding—a reunion of sorts with all that was once comfortable and familiar.

I felt like a real adult at the wedding because although my parents were there, I was at my own table far away from them. Plus, with the *Full House* cast and crew on hand, I had more friends in one room than I usually did so I was fairly comfortable.

It had the potential to be a great day. And, let's not get selfish here, for Candace and her husband, hockey star Valeri Bure, it was probably the best day of their lives. For me, with my hair up, a little black dress hugging my hips, and Ryan (my first real boyfriend) on my arm, it was time to party.

Ryan was one of the more popular kids and my link to an

elevated high school social status. He was a junior and I was a freshman. (That right there was an accomplishment in its own right. Go me!) Everyone at school liked him, even though he was known as the class clown and wasn't exactly on the honor roll. He's probably a senator now or something. Ryan was certainly not a Boy Scout so of course my dad hated him. My mom tried to be supportive of me. I think she was just happy that I had a boyfriend.

Ryan and I both decided that the wedding was going to be a lot of fun. Our definitions of fun, though, turned out to be quite different.

While we sat at our very adult table, the waiter came around with the red wine. He didn't card anyone or ever question how old we were. I had sipped some champagne at *Full House* wrap parties before, but this glass of wine was my first real drink. I downed the whole glass. I felt a rush of energy course through my body. I instantly felt like a new person. That first drink gave me the self-confidence I had been searching for all this time. That first drink, that was it—the key to everything I was missing in life.

The waiter was still pouring wine for the other people at the table when I finished the first glass. When he made his way back to me, I was ready for round two.

"Don't you think you should slow down?" Ryan asked. For all his bad-boy ways he wasn't much of a drinker.

"No, I'm good."

"What if your mom finds out?"

"Don't worry about it," I said, positive that I could hide it. "She won't know."

"OK. If you say so."

That one drink gave me the upper hand. It immediately made me the decision maker. It let me be the person I wanted to be.

The first drink led to the second drink and to the third, fourth, fifth, and, well, I lost count there. I couldn't drink it quickly enough. The drinking became my focus for the night and nothing was going to stand in my way. I finally felt comfortable in my own skin. All my worries had been washed away.

The first time you drink you have no idea how to drink or what will happen anyway, so you just keep drinking and drinking and you swear you're not drunk. Everyone knew I was drinking but the others at my table weren't paying attention to how much I'd downed, and the other cast members were focused on having their own fun. With my parents on the other side of the room, all I really had was Ryan, who at this point was probably wishing he were somewhere else.

"Oh, shit," he said when he saw that I was absolutely plastered. Most of the evening from that point on is a blur. Turns out, I would always be a blackout drinker, who, only through a handful of disturbing clues, could piece a night together.

All I can remember was feeling like absolute hell. Ryan took me outside for some air. I was out of my mind, leaning against the wall of a beautiful country club. The world was spinning. The vomit was on its way. I ran into the bathroom and puked all over the place; regurgitated red wine all over the fancy bathroom. I was so embarrassed.

My mom came in and was mortified. Then Andrea Barber and her mom, Sherry, came in. More embarrassment. Others from the show followed. They sat me up in a chair and put my head in a trash can. I fell over, hit my head on the metal bin, scored a giant bruise across my nose, and passed out on the floor.

Darkness.

From there, I was later told, Jono, one of Candace's friends (who years later would pitch networks the idea for a Jodie Sweetin reality show) entered the women's bathroom and carried me out to the backseat of my parents' car. Pretty. Fucking. Embarrassing.

The barfing continued during the car ride and then I was finally in the comfort of my own home. My parents were furious with me. Parents hate to see their kids royally fucked up in front of a large group of people.

The next morning I was hungover, swearing I would never drink again and begging for forgiveness from my parents. I was truly sorry, but at the same time, I had found the key to being more confident, funnier, and self-assured. A big chunk that I felt was missing in me had been filled that day by drinking.

At that wedding, with the alcohol, I wasn't a kid in high school who struggled to fit in. I wasn't Stephanie Tanner. I wasn't the actor who played Stephanie Tanner. I was Jodie Sweetin and I was an alcoholic.

chapter eight

DRUNK AND HIGH SCHOOL

candace's wedding was in June 1996, the end of my freshman year of high school. From that day on, I was a different person, drinking as often as possible— usually a couple times a week. It wasn't that drinking made me popular, but it gave me a confidence to be cool. It sounds silly, but at fourteen, I needed that extra something to make me feel comfortable around other kids my age.

And it was that easy. During my sophomore year, I became closer with the cheerleaders, the jocks, and the kids in the accelerated classes with the brains, the looks, and the money. They were cool. And that's what I wanted.

Of course moving toward the cool crowd alienates many other people and the typical high school cattiness soon followed. Plus, within my new group of friends, there was a lot of jealousy, rivalry, and cliques. It's a constant battle inside the high school world. Only the strong survive.

To ensure I had a chance to make it out alive I wore what the popular kids wore, talked like them, and made sure I had the same interests and hobbies. Even if I wasn't really into whatever it was that they deemed cool, I could fake it. I am an actor after all.

So I listened to Smashing Pumpkins, bought a bunch of trendy necklaces, and hung out on Main Street in Huntington Beach. I wanted to be like everyone else.

Before, I had to blend in to prove that I didn't think I was better than other people. People thought I was stuck-up because of my TV role, so I did whatever it took to make friends and be liked.

No matter what I did then, it wasn't good enough for other people. No matter how hard I campaigned for friends, it didn't work. If I talked to everyone in the class, people said I talked too much. If I sat in the back of the class and didn't talk to anyone, people said I had a bad attitude.

I couldn't win.

How could I have friends without looking like I was trying too hard? How could I keep to myself without people thinking I was a snob? I looked around and thought my classmates had it together, that they had something I didn't. I wanted to figure out how to be more like them.

The answer: alcohol . . . and drugs.

I started going to all the parties and sneaking alcohol when I would go out with school friends, chasing that feeling I had at the wedding. I found friends who would steal alcohol with me from other parents' liquor cabinets, sneak cigarettes, and do other things that were considered breaking the rules.

My parents were not pleased. I lied to them often and every now and then they would catch me. My parents weren't drinkers. They didn't have alcohol in the house. They knew the drinking and the partying was taking place outside their fence, so they slapped a curfew on me, told me who I could and couldn't hang out with, and watched my every move as much as they could. It wasn't enough.

Ryan, as much of a badass as he was, wasn't a fan of what I was turning into. He was a problem in his own right— getting into fights at football games and flooding the school auditorium in a senior prank gone bad—but he didn't drink or party, so when we went to a Winter Formal and I was drinking in the limo—from a flask—he wasn't happy. He tried to stop me from drinking, which wasn't fun for either one of us. I found the fun people who would have the kind of night that I enjoyed and I left him behind. He tried to save me and keep me from hanging out with the wrong crowd, but that was a decision I had already made. That was where I wanted to go.

I needed to drink and I was going to do it as often as possible regardless of what he or my parents said or did. I knew that as long as I could check out mentally with alcohol, I could fit in better and not worry so much about what I felt inside. Every time I drank, I would remember the feeling at the wedding. I wanted that rush back, but could never find it again. I didn't know then that that's the thing with addiction: no high is ever as good as it is the first time.

When chasing that high, there is a natural progression when it comes to substance abuse: after alcohol, comes pot.

It was a bright, sunny California day. I was a fifteen-year-old high school junior and Nicole, a popular girl in my grade who lived around the corner from me, picked me up in the morning, as she did every morning, to drive me to school. Nicole smoked pot all the time, but on this sunny morning, she invited me to join in.

"You want a hit?" she asked as she blew out the smoke and put her hands back on the wheel.

"Um, sure why not," I said, taking the little pipe from her hand.

"Do you know what you are doing?"

"I can do this," I muttered under my breath.

I fumbled with the pipe, didn't even know how to light it, and in an attempt to smoke it, I blew pot all over the car.

"What the hell did you just do?" Nicole yelled.

"I-I don't know."

"Oh, Jodes, first timer, huh?"

Just outside the school parking lot she pulled over and showed me how it was done. I never really liked smoking pot. It just made me tired and hungry at the end. I did it because it was there and because it made me feel like I could escape and be someone else just for a while.

* * *

Though I may have been a clumsy smoker, I was a pretty slick drunk. I was still able to be the kid that got good grades and was polite and lovable around my parents and other family members.

I quickly developed dual personalities—the good girl and the bad girl—that I could switch on and off depending on the situation.

But one thing changed. All of a sudden I was drinking more than everyone else at these high school parties. I was partying harder and was more obsessed with getting fucked up. Other kids were rebelling against their families and experimenting like normal high school kids. I was out of control. Even from the very beginning, one drink wasn't enough. Others were happy being buzzed. I needed to be completely smashed and obliterated.

I wanted to prove that I wasn't the girl from *Full House*, that I could get more trashed than everybody else and be the complete opposite of what people expected from Stephanie Tanner. I was going to be the antithesis of that character. That was my goal.

The whole cast had gone in different directions at this point. Candace became a great wife and mother and focused on her faith. The Olsens created a giant empire with films, clothing lines, and a number of business ventures. If *Full House* was like a real family, then I was destined to be the black sheep. That was my way of separating myself from the pack—I'd be the fuckup. It's not exactly what I had planned, but that's the way it was.

By my senior year I was pretty out of control, but I felt like I had friends. Drinking made me fun and fun equaled friendship.

As my drinking continued, I started getting into more trouble at school. Once, I was in photo class and was supposed to walk around campus with a classmate to shoot industrial shots—chain-link fences, pipes, wires, that kind of thing. We were taking photos of a high-voltage outage box and noticed that the padlock was undone, so we went inside. The rebellious bug inside of me came out immediately. I looked around for security cameras, pulled the electric switches down, and ran. Pretending as though nothing happened, we went about our business taking photos, as students and teachers started clearing out of the school. We laughed hysterically when we realized that we had turned off the power in the entire building. The only problem: we had taken photos of the whole affair. Evidence. A couple of weeks later another friend developed the shots, blew them up, and gave them to me, but no one turned me in.

Then, just before the end of the school year, I went out one night with a group of friends, got really drunk, and toilet papered some poor girl's house. We did the damage and drove off but the cops caught up to us. I wasn't behind the wheel but I was by far the drunkest in the car. When the cops stopped us, I literally fell out of the car and started puking everywhere. Somehow, that made me seem guilty. The cops called my parents who came and picked me up. Again, my mom was furious. This time, she promised to punish me.

"You're not going to Grad Night," she yelled, threatening to take away the most important night of my life.

"But you don't understand," I told her. "It's the most important night of my life. I can't miss it."

She caved. I went, but promised to be good.

On Grad Night—an all-night party inside the school gym—my friends and I decided to bond over a little Ecstasy. Did I promise to be good? Oh well. So a group of us who had never done it before took Ecstasy and rolled our faces off. The chaperones at this little party had no clue but we had the time of our lives. We danced for eight hours straight. Then I felt the need to go up to every person I knew and apologize for random things that occurred throughout high school. Drugs can make you open up that way, I guess. Everyone seemed to have so much to say. It lasted all night.

At 6:30 a.m. the following morning, our parents were supposed to come pick us up. It felt like the end of *The Breakfast Club*, where everyone goes back with his or her parents and reality sets in. The only difference was that my mom didn't show. Still pissed off at the Great Drunken Toilet Papering of 1999, my mom chose not to pick me up. It was a bit embarrassing, but I had a friend take me home, where I stumbled to my bedroom, passed out in my clothes, and slept the rest of the day.

In just four years of high school, I went from an innocent little girl afraid to break the rules to the complete opposite of what anyone had expected—the anti-Stephanie. Had they given out superlatives in elementary school I would have been voted most likely to succeed (or, at least, cutest smile).

But in high school, all I got was "worst driver," since I was known to drive fast, and sometimes drunk, in my BMW 328.

All that grief and my parents still threw me a kick-ass graduation party. Can you believe it? I was really some sort of con artist back then. Either that, or they just wanted me to be happy.

The graduation party was amazing. We had a deejay spinning in the backyard and all my friends came. And even better, the whole *Full House* cast came, too, which excited many of my friends. The highlight of this fabulous soiree was, of course, John Stamos and his wife at the time, Rebecca Romijn. They were the life of the party and also the last people to leave. She was dancing with a bunch of my guy friends and just like that, I became the coolest person in the world. Who needs drugs when you have Rebecca Romijn?

chapter nine

OUT OF CONTROL

the summer between high school and college I
was glued to my new boyfriend's side. We met in March, just
a couple of months before I graduated. Candace and I had
gone to Arrowhead Pond in Anaheim to watch her husband
and the Calgary Flames take on the Mighty Ducks. I wasn't
much of a hockey fan, but I figured a night out with Candace would be a good break from the high school crowd.
After the game, we were backstage (back ice? whatever they
call it) and this guy walked by—almost as if in slow motion—and our eyes locked.

He sent his friend over and since I was with Candace
and her husband, I figured they were looking for autographs
or a photo or something. But instead, he told me that his
friend thought I was cute and wanted my number.

That was a nice surprise. Eventually, he came over and

started talking to me. He was a handsome, twenty-year-old security guard at the arena named Shaun Holguin. He didn't know anything about *Full House*. To him, I was just some girl at a hockey game and I liked that. I took his number and waited almost a month to call him. I had never met a guy outside of school before, so it seemed awkward and a little scary to pick up the phone. But my mom pushed me into it, and Shaun and I talked for hours before planning a first date.

The first date led to the second and by the fall, I had a boyfriend whenever I needed him. When I left for Chapman University with my capri pants and Dave Matthews Band CD (it was 1999—don't judge), I was happy to have him on the side, for when I felt like being a girlfriend. I was happier, though, that he was willing to take a backseat and wait for me to mature.

I originally thought about being a film major because I thought that seemed like a good next step. I didn't particularly want to direct or produce films, but it was the only thing close to what I knew and I didn't want to major in drama or theater. I had goals in the beginning, which was good, but once I was at school that changed.

As you can imagine, my parents were not too happy with me going off on my own. Luckily for them, Chapman was all of twenty minutes from my house. Still, I was living on my own and prone to partying—a recipe for disaster.

They fought me on living there at first, but my parents made me a deal: I could live on campus, as long as I came home on the weekends. Instead of on-campus living working to my benefit—teaching me how to take care of myself and about responsibility—I ended up partying all week and well, that's about it. I didn't do anything else. I didn't go to classes. I didn't do anything but go out all night and sleep all day.

I was drinking heavily, doing Ecstasy, smoking pot, and using pretty much anything else I could get my hands on. I would come home Friday afternoon and sleep until Sunday, when it was time to head back to school.

My parents knew something was up but they had no idea how bad it was getting. They probably assumed I was drinking a little but they never would have guessed the extent to which I was doing drugs and missing classes. They questioned me, but they took my word for it. I was in college and becoming an adult. There was only so much that they could do—until my grades came out.

It was during this period that I snorted cocaine for the first time. I was in a friend's dorm room and a bunch of us were going to some underground club in downtown LA. We were all getting ready to go and someone had it. "Oh sweet," I thought. "I've never tried that before." I was ready to party.

Doing coke was a big deal for all of us. It wasn't like the Hollywood scene where no one thinks twice about doing lines off the back of a toilet. At the time, it was a line that most college students in Orange County didn't cross very often. Even so, out of the four or five people in the group, everyone else had already tried it before. It was my first time, and it was a life-changing moment for me.

Instead of being nervous I was all too happy to find a new high. I watched the others do it first. Inhale through the straw—seems easy enough. It wasn't like that first time smoking pot. There was no real way to screw this up.

So I did a line.

It was a huge rush. I felt taller, better looking, and excited to party. I wanted to listen to really loud music and dance until the sun came up. Physically, I had the energy of Wonder Woman and emotionally, I felt more connected to the world, closer to my friends, and at peace with life. It was total euphoria—for the first few hours, at least.

We headed to the underground club, but as it turned out, I was the only one underage and couldn't get in. Stuck in downtown LA, I decided to drive back to the dorms. But the long trip back wasn't good for my mental state. Coming down off the coke, I was crying, depressed, and doubting every decision I'd ever made in my life. I thought coke was the worst drug I'd ever tried.

Back at the dorms, I started to wonder if this small bit of sadness would lift if I did more coke. I knew where to find it. I went to the dorm room where the night began, found the bag with the leftover coke, and, alone in the room, finished it—four lines right in a row—before I roamed the campus for another party.

It got me through the night.

I didn't like cocaine the first few times I did it. It was good for a little while but then a terrible feeling and period of depression would come over me. I kept doing it anyway. My friends loved it and I knew if I kept trying, I could enjoy it the same way they did. Sometimes other people had it, sometimes it was my idea to go out and get it. Either way, the times I did coke in college led to the destruction that would follow years later.

Because coke wasn't as easy to get my hands on in college, I stuck mostly to alcohol and the things college kids were into like Ecstasy and pot. I was drunk or high most of the time and the lifestyle was wearing on me. I started looking pale and thin, and my parents were concerned that they had completely lost control over me.

My schoolwork was also suffering. I needed help. My freshman seminar professor saw that I was having problems. I'd call him and tell him I couldn't make it to a test and he'd have me come to his office to work on the material. He sat me down and talked to me, trying to get to the root of my problems since he knew I was a good student at heart. I tried to cover up the fact that I was partying hard by acting as if I just didn't understand the material. There was nothing he could do. With a dismal 0.9 GPA, I was on academic probation and close to failing out.

Depression set in.

I tried to stop drinking. I knew I should try to pull myself together and go to class. But when I'd quit drinking for a week, I'd end up smoking more pot. I couldn't stop, and the truth is I didn't want to. Partying kept me from thinking and feeling bad about myself, which was a good thing because when I had too much going on in my head, bad things happened.

I knew a couple of girls who were cutters—they would take razors to their arms and slice themselves open. They enjoyed the pain and got high off the sight of the blood. I thought, "I wonder if that works."

I had a toolbox in my dorm with a straight razor in it. I wanted to feel something so badly that I sat down in my dorm-room closet and decided to try it.

I had been drinking heavily.

I looked down and I was bleeding all down my arm. I put a sweatshirt on and ran from my fourth-floor room to my friend's room on the first floor. I pulled up the sleeve of my sweatshirt.

"I think this is bad," I said with a hint of fear in my drunken slurred voice.

"What the fuck were you doing?"

"I don't know. I just don't know."

She laid me down on the bed and I passed out. The next day I woke up, looked down at my arm, and realized I hadn't solved anything—I'd made it worse. But at the same time the cuts seemed like an outlet for my emotional pain. It was like a physical expression of my inner turmoil—all the pain I'd buried about feeling so very alone; I couldn't feel it anymore, but I could at least see it.

I tried cutting three or four more times. Nothing deep, just little scratches on my forearm or on the palm of my hand with a straight razor blade. I did it when I was absolutely hammered. Somehow it released this pain I had inside and made me feel better. But it was hard to hide and I didn't need people asking about the cuts on my arms. Alcohol and drugs were much easier to cover up.

Around the same time, I was partying at a hotel in Newport Beach. I was so coked up that I was standing on the ledge of the fourth- or fifth-story balcony, like Jenny from *Forrest Gump*. I decided to climb up to the top rung of a nearby fire-escape ladder. I don't remember what I was thinking but when I got down, I didn't need a friend to ask me, "What the fuck were you doing?" I knew on my own; things were bad.

During this downward spiral, Shaun was really concerned about me. My roommate Nancy would call him all the time, worried because I was missing. He lived fairly close to school so on a day when I thought I should be sober I would crash at his house in an attempt to get my life together.

Shaun wasn't a really social person and he hated my friends, but I wanted to see him more often. I'd try to get him to be like me, to go out and have fun. I'd bring him along to college parties, but that never worked out.

At one fraternity party, I ended up on the curb across the street throwing up in the gutter. He carried me three blocks to my dorm and put me in bed. He stayed for a while and when I fell asleep he thought I was passed out for the night, so he left. I woke up an hour later and went back out to party.

Clubbing with Shaun was a disaster. I brought him out with my college friends to one club, but because he was wearing a T-shirt, he didn't get in. "Oh, that's too bad," I said with one foot inside the club. "See you later." I ditched him, which by itself was terrible. But even worse: his car keys were in my purse.

I popped Ecstasy into my mouth and was ready to party. Shaun tried calling me but I couldn't hear my phone. He sat on his car outside the club for two hours and was not happy.

When I walked outside later, I was stunned to see him.

"What are you doing here?" I asked, trying to act like I wasn't on drugs.

"You have my keys," he said, fighting any urge to lose his cool.

After a deep breath he drove me back to the dorms and planned to hang out. I decided I wasn't quite done partying. I told him I would be back in a minute and went to a friend's room to do lines of coke. Moments later, he came banging on the door. I ran to a closet—bringing the coke with me—while my friend tried to hold him off. He yelled and eventually stormed off. I finished the coke and went after him. We screamed at each other in the street. I knew I was wrong but I still put up a fight. He peeled off in his big Ford Bronco and threatened to never talk to me again.

The next day, with tears running down my face, I promised to stop doing drugs. I said I would clean up my act, become a different person. I wasn't just doing it for Shaun. I knew I was headed down a bad path. I had to get out of Chapman's dorms, but first I had to tell my parents.

Shaun and I were at a Carl's Jr. deciding how I would break it to my parents that I had a drug problem and needed to move home. Tears were still flowing. I didn't want to do it. I went into the bathroom and when I returned, Shaun was holding the open phone in his hand. He had called my mom and told her everything.

I took the phone—balling, apologetic—and talked to my mom. I was ready to start a new phase of my life.

I moved back with my parents and commuted to school. I had to pull myself together because I was running out of options and knew I was ruining my life. I started going to a recovery program and attempted to get my life in order. It had to be done, but I wasn't fully ready. I went to the meetings, but I didn't take the steps seriously. At that point I was dry but not sober, but for those sixteen months at home, I lived in my bubble and stayed clean and focused on school.

During this attempt to clean up, Shaun and I grew closer. Having a real relationship was difficult since we both lived with our parents. He wasn't even allowed to be in my room. It was like high school. I thought that would be a deal breaker for him but we made it work. His house was better— his mom would let me sleep there. Still, it was frustrating, both mentally and, well, sexually.

Over that time I also grew really close to his family. His mom was like Wonder Wife: she volunteered at the drop of a hat, cooked big meals for everyone, and even sewed curtains. I wished I had her energy. I saw what a happy, domestic lifestyle looked like. That was what I wanted.

My mom had all the same characteristics but I didn't appreciate that as much, then. Once I started spending time with Shaun's family, though, I started to reconnect with my parents.

I began wanting to become more of a family person, more of an adult. I knew Shaun was the guy to help make it happen. He was to be my saving grace from the mess my life had become. He was there for me and he would protect me from going back to using. I didn't realize that I was setting myself up for an unhealthy, codependent relationship.

Deep down, I looked at him as a parent, not as my partner. He was someone I had to answer to. I felt like I had to change and be someone else with him. Looking back now, I realize I didn't need to be completely different—just sober.

But I wasn't ready and I thought he was the answer. He was going to help me turn the page on that terrible time in college. He was going to pick up the pieces. With Shaun, I would be safe.

chapter ten

LOVE AND MARRIAGE

when i lived at home, Shaun became my life. All my
free time was spent eating dinner at his parents' house, going
to movies, and having low-key nights with him.

My world suddenly became a lot smaller: Shaun, my parents, and a couple of friends—that was it. Because I had decided to stop using drugs and alcohol, I lost most of the
friends who had continued to use. They had a constant party
going and I no longer wanted to be a part of it.

Marriage seemed like the logical next step. We both
wanted it. We talked about it for a little while—where we
would live, how our life together would be—then went ring
shopping in downtown LA and had the ring designed. Before
I knew it, we were searching for wedding locations.

One afternoon in May 2001, we were standing at the
pool deck on top of the Casa Del Mar in Santa Monica. The

sun was setting over the beach. It was beautiful. I definitely thought this was a place where we could get married. He seemed to agree but he was acting strangely quiet, even for him.

He was nervous, shaking.

"What's wrong with you?" I asked. "Don't you like this place?"

"Yeah, it's great," he said. "Will you marry me?"

He didn't get down on one knee and he didn't have some whole speech prepared, but when that ring came out I screamed in excitement. Even though I knew we were going to get married and that it was only a matter of time before he put a ring on it, I was still stunned. Tears of joy ran down my face.

We got to the car and I immediately called my mom.

"Oh my God, Mom, he asked me to marry him," I shrilled with joy. She joined in. I think her prayers were answered. Even though I was nineteen, she and I both thought this was exactly what I needed to turn my life around. We went back to my house and took photos with my parents.

"Everything is going to be perfect now," I thought.

My mom, who had been doing some work as a wedding coordinator, was off and running once we broke the news. She had a vision for the wedding. I had a vision for my new life.

Candace got married young, had kids, and lived in a nice house in a good neighborhood. She wasn't passing out at fraternity parties. She was cooking, helping kids with homework—adult things. That's what I wanted.

When some of my friends called me crazy for getting engaged so young, Candace offered sage advice: "Don't listen to them. If you are happy that's all that matters. Val and I have done it for years and we're really happy. You can be, too."

She was the closest thing I had to a sister so I asked her to be my matron of honor and her daughter to be my flower girl.

A month after we got engaged Shaun and I moved into a house in Rossmoor, an area of Orange County near my parents. Even though it had a white picket fence, our dream home needed some work; we needed to gut and remodel it.

We spent the next year planning the wedding and creating the perfect living environment. We worked with an interior designer and walked around Home Depot. Instead of partying, that was what we did for fun. The house was done in bright yellows and deep blues and had a French country look to it, which opened the door to a lot of floral patterns, the only thing he'd fight against. He wasn't a fan, but we compromised. Shaun had one room—the back corner bedroom—where he could do whatever he wanted. It looked like a hunting lodge: everything was forest green. He had his guitars and a big TV in there and both he and our bulldog, Norman, called that room home.

We got Norman when we first moved in together. He and Ginger, a Yorkshire terrier he had given me as a Christmas present in 2000, were our babies. We felt like a little family and talked about having children of our own. We decided that we'd wait a few years since we were still young, but it was something we both wanted.

I cooked dinner and settled into life as a homemaker. I planted roses out front and nestled into a part I knew I could play.

We spent so much time focusing on fixing up the house and arranging our new life that we didn't have time for much else. I was also focused on school and the wedding, and he was working his way through the police academy. Shaun was a musician on the side and played bass in a band with his friends, so occasionally we would go scope out the competition or watch one of his friends play. We also had a twenty-eight-foot travel trailer that we took camping in Yosemite or Sequoia National Park, or to the beach. But on most Saturday nights, we just went to a movie or ordered takeout. In order to stay sober, I thought I was better off keeping things low-key, and because Shaun was a homebody, he liked that plan.

There were times, though, when it wasn't enough. Feeling like I needed a social life and was losing my connection with college, I decided to rush the Alpha Phi sorority. But there was a lot of drinking involved in sorority life and mandatory meetings every Monday—two things I wasn't interested in. I dropped out before I really got started.

It was a big step for me to turn down joining a group of girls that liked to drink. I thought I had kicked the habit. I was in a 12-step program, but I was operating on my own schedule. As I said, I was "dry" but not "sober," since I didn't take the necessary steps dictated by the program to help myself. After my victory of saying no to the sorority, I stopped going to meetings and started doubting that I really was an alcoholic. After all, I thought I was too young to be a *real* alcoholic.

My bachelorette party went off without a cocktail in sight. Candace, the other bridesmaids, and I all went to Benihana in Beverly Hills. The girls brought sex toys and passed them out to random people in the restaurant instructing them to come up to me and say, "Excuse me, is this yours?" Throughout the dinner, strangers came up to me handing me pink dildos or fuzzy handcuffs, while little kids sat right across from me. I was so embarrassed, but it was a lot of fun.

Shaun didn't have your typical wild bachelor party. His brother organized a stripper-free golf getaway . . . at least that's what I was told.

As our wedding approached it seemed like we were both on the same page, but a part of me wondered if we were both just on his.

On July 27, 2002, friends, family, and the entire *Full House* cast, as well as producers and directors, came together for my dream wedding. The service was at The First Congregational Church of Los Angeles, a huge, beautiful Gothic cathedral in downtown LA. We had 170 people, but the church sat 1,200 so it looked almost empty. There was a giant pipe organ and beautiful flowers everywhere. It was as traditional as it gets and when they played the wedding march, I appeared in a custom-made, champagne duchess silk Eve of Milady ball gown, with a tiara and jewels and a fifteen-foot-long cathedral train. All in all it was a fifteen-thousand-dollar getup, but I felt like a million-dollar bride. It was an absolute dream moment.

I looked down the aisle and saw Shaun and my brides-maids—friends from college or childhood—and a sister who played one on TV and who fit the role perfectly on this per-fect day.

My dad walked me down the aisle and at first he was teary-eyed which was cute. Then he got nervous or some-thing, because he wouldn't stop talking. The whole walk (and it was a long one) was "Did you see so-and-so?" and "Oh, that's nice that so-and-so is here," 120 feet of constant chatter.

I wanted to tell him to just shut up already, but it actu-ally helped that he was so chatty. In the moments of silence, I started to get nervous. All of a sudden, thoughts began racing through my head. This was a huge decision and this long walk down the aisle was giving me way too much time to think.

"Oh, my God, what am I doing?"

"Is this what I want?"

"What have I done?"

"Ahhhhhhh!"

With the butterflies in my stomach, the voices in my head, and my dad being dad, it's a miracle I didn't bolt out of there.

But the ceremony went off without a hitch and when it was over I let out a big sigh of relief. The reception moved to the Casa Del Mar, where we had gotten engaged not so long ago. It's a beautiful hotel, one of the best in the world.

There, we had violinists and a live rock band. There were roses everywhere; crystal votive candleholders for each place setting; and, for all the women, gold slippers, with Shaun's name and mine in ribbon, so they could take off their shoes and dance.

It was an amazing day. It was the best party I had ever been to. Ever. It was my day and I loved it.

As the night came to a close, Shaun and I sat and reflected on how perfect it all was. The catering manager saw my happiness and approached me.

I was twenty years old, underage, and a recovering alcoholic, but he didn't know that last part. He saw me having the time of my life on the most special day of my life, with all the people I loved and who loved me. He saw my smile and thought he could add to the fun.

"If you want us to sneak you champagne, we can give you some," he said with a smile.

"No thanks," I said. "I don't drink."

chapter eleven

A TALE OF TWO PERSONALITIES

married life was pretty darn good at first. We took off to Tahiti for eight days on an amazing honeymoon. We flew into Papeete and were supposed to take a shuttle flight to Bora Bora. Because our flight was late getting in, we missed the shuttle, but I refused to miss out on Bora Bora. We managed to wrangle a few other couples into putting money together to charter a flight there.

In Bora Bora, we had a room on stilts over the water with a glass-bottom floor. We snorkeled and relaxed in the sun and did, you know, the stuff that married people do. ("Our taxes," as they would say on *Full House*.) It was beautiful and very relaxing. I came back to Southern California with my hair sun bleached blonde and my skin as dark as Donatella Versace's.

Once the vacation was over we were back to our home,

our life, and it wasn't long before it became clear that the honeymoon was over.

I loved Shaun very much. There was never a point when I didn't love him. But the life I was living—a sober housewife finishing school without any social life—wasn't what I wanted. I was too young, too immature. I started to get that restless and irritable feeling that comes when I'm in a place where I'm not secure in my sobriety.

Three months into my marriage, Halloween rolled around and my friend Kristen invited me to a murder-mystery party boat. It sounded fun, but more important, it sounded like an opportunity to drink.

Kristen liked to party and her boyfriend was a bartender on the boat. All the pieces were falling into place. I knew what I was getting myself into. The night before the party, my mind was going 90 mph thinking about how I was going to pull it off, how I was going to orchestrate the situation to allow myself to drink: when it would happen, how it would happen, where it would happen. I couldn't get to it quickly enough. In my head, I was drinking the day before I picked up the first cocktail.

I wasn't an alcoholic, I told myself. I was just too young before to know how to control my drinking. This time, I thought, I could control it. Given the amount of preparation and obsession I was putting into this first drink, that was clearly not the case.

The boat set sail out of Newport Beach and I was halfway through dinner when I casually ordered a glass of champagne.

Kristen looked at me funny. She had known me since high school and knew some of my struggles. But I downplayed it.

"It's cool," I assured her. "I can totally handle it."

Inside, I could have jumped up in excitement and danced on a chair at just the sight of it. The first sip was so warm, bubbly, delicious. I held it in my mouth for a second, closed my eyes blissfully, and swallowed. It hit my stomach and the bubbles when straight to my head. I didn't want any more dinner or some murder mystery. I wanted a cigarette, a bottle of champagne, and a Jack Daniel's and Coke to wash it down.

Kristen didn't know what she was getting herself into. All of a sudden I was fourteen again, sitting at an adult table at Candace's wedding. A couple drinks in and there was no stopping me. By the end of the boat ride, I was hammered and couldn't care less about who killed whom with the lead pipe in the library.

After the boat docked we decided to head up to Sunset Boulevard to look for trouble. Kristen was driving at this point because I could barely speak coherently.

Shaun called. It was 3:30 a.m.

"Where the hell are you?"

I put Kristen on the phone. "We're up in LA. I'll have Jodie home soon."

He was furious.

I was sick to my stomach. I enjoyed the night to a point, but then excitement turned to disappointment. On the way home I was completely guilt ridden, sobbing uncontrollably.

I had overshot the mark. I didn't want to come home the blubbering, drunken, passed-out idiot. I couldn't believe I had gotten to that point.

When I got home all I could do was apologize. I knew I screwed up. I knew I would never be able to justify that I'd drank again.

I vomited, then crawled into bed. I couldn't stop thinking, going back and forth in my mind, fighting to suppress the feeling of drunken joy and loving the feeling of euphoria at the same time. I knew it was wrong, but to me it felt right. I knew there was no turning back.

When the smoke cleared with Shaun, I decided I would try to include Shaun in my drinking and we would both feel as if we'd won. I cooked dinner every night and we had dinner parties at our house on the weekends, so I thought I could add alcohol to the equation and be just fine.

Shaun wasn't opposed to it because at least he would be there to watch me drink. He could make sure it was a casual thing and not a problem. He'd have preferred that I didn't drink at all, but if I had to, it would be under his watch. He could limit the number of drinks.

I knew it opened the door.

The first dinner went smoothly. I had a few glasses of wine and everything seemed OK. Shaun was still concerned, but there was no harm done this time around as far as he knew. Inside of me, it was just like the murder-mystery boat—plotting, obsessing over that first drink.

We decided to get into wines. That's how Shaun was. He didn't just go mountain biking, he became a mountain-biking enthusiast. Same thing with wine; he wasn't going to just drink a red with dinner, he was going to become a wine expert.

I knew this was my in, my way to manipulate the situation. For Christmas I got him a *Wine for Dummies* book.

Just like that I was back in.

For Shaun's sake, I talked the talk. I'd work "I hear a '78 Cabernet from Italy is divine"—or something like that—into conversation. I walked the walk. I cooked pasta and chicken for dinner, watched him bring out a bottle, and didn't bat an eye.

It was perfect.

But as we drank more together, Shaun started getting concerned. He started to cut me off.

I hated it.

I couldn't get enough and I didn't need him limiting my drinking. He wasn't my dad, and it wasn't his choice.

I started to hide the alcohol from him. At first I'd hide my drinking right in front of him. We'd go out and he'd set a limit of three drinks. I'd have the three and then, when he wasn't looking, I'd sneak in a few shots. But I wanted more and I knew where to go.

I reconnected with the people I knew in high school and college who were doing drugs. Although some of them were better and had moved on from that scene, I kept dropping hints about getting back into partying. Eventually, I found a group of people—including Monica who had gone to rehab for speed back in high school—with whom I could spend my nights.

I went with Monica and her brothers to play pool one night in Long Beach. We were drinking pretty heavily and became friendly with the guys at the table next to us. From the pool hall we moved the party to their house. They were drug-dealing, welfare-living people who lived in their grandmother's house with pit bulls chained to the front gate. They sat on the porch smoking blunts and shooting dice. Their neighbor was a thirteen-year-old kid who sold drugs—a common occurrence since kids, when caught, can be sent only to a juvenile detention center. I knew these were the kind of people I could party with. That first night there we sat around drinking, smoking pot, listening to music. We had little in common but the weed and booze. We partied until 3:00 a.m. and then I raced home to beat Shaun back.

Shaun worked twelve-hour shifts at the police department, mostly at night, so my schedule was usually clear. At first I just went out drinking and made sure to beat him home. But it was a lot harder to hide drinking than drugs because I'd reek of alcohol after a night out. I couldn't give up that feeling of being high or of sneaking around and getting away with it. So, instead of the heavy drinking I moved on to coke and Ecstasy—no muss, no fuss. It quickly became an everyday habit.

Shaun would leave at 5:00 p.m., I'd head out to party by 9:00 or 10:00 p.m. and race home by 4:00 a.m., so I could be in bed, pretending to be asleep, when he walked in at 5:00 a.m. I'd wait for him to pass out and then I would get up and go about my day until I crashed. It was a terrible routine, but for a while it worked.

* * *

I started hanging out with the guys from Long Beach regularly, without Monica. I stayed connected to them and kept them separate from my life with Shaun. I could go to that world when I wanted to.

One night while I was there, they started talking about meth. Methamphetamines are psychostimulants that speed up the heart rate, create a state of intense euphoria, and ultimately are extremely addictive. I knew all of that, but I didn't care.

The group was talking about how great their night had been because of it and about all the fun times they had had with it. When I mentioned that I'd never done it, everyone seemed surprised and acted as if doing meth was not a big deal, like taking your first sip of alcohol. We all know how well I handled that experience, so I knew meth was going to send me down the wrong path. I didn't care.

I was searching for a new high and wanted to have the kind of fun everyone was talking about. I was excited.

We bought some off the thirteen-year-old next door and I couldn't get to it fast enough. I snorted it and my nose felt like it was on fire. It was the worst burning sensation ever, but it was the single most exhilarating experience of my life up till then. I felt invincible, like I could do anything. I felt like the best-looking, funniest, most perfect person I could be. It was similar to the way I had felt when I had my first drink and first line of coke, but this—this was one thousand times better.

Everything was great that night until I went home. My husband was lying next to me in bed and I was terrified that he could hear my heart beating. It was beating so hard and so fast, like it was beating out of my chest. I thought I was going to die of a heart attack in the middle of the night. My heart was pounding, my pupils were the size of dinner plates, and my thoughts were racing 1,000 mph. I was all over the place. How was I going to be able to hide this? Hours went by before I eventually passed out. But I didn't get caught.

In a short time, I went from being scared of getting caught to being totally confident that I could add meth to the menu without Shaun ever noticing.

Within a month I was doing meth all the time. I had a new group of friends who did it with me, and I dropped a lot of weight. I thought I looked better and felt better than ever before. It was all fun and exciting, so different from the normal, housewife life I had been living up until that point. I no longer felt like the boring, mature version of me that I didn't find interesting or particularly like.

Meth helped me escape my head and bury my anxiety. Sober, I didn't know where I wanted to go or what to do with my life; with meth I didn't care. I didn't worry about what I wasn't, I just thought about how I was going to get high next.

I was spending about five hundred dollars a week on meth at this point, but Shaun never suspected anything. His job paid for most of the bills, and because I handled his paychecks and the household finances I got good at shuffling things around so he wouldn't know money was disappearing.

Shaun never looked at our finances and never questioned me. Nobody ever questioned my behavior.

I convinced my parents that I had lost weight from working out and was tired from all the work I was doing around the house. I was even able to fool a psychiatrist into believing that I was depressed and needed medication, which I told sober friends was the reason I was suddenly losing weight. The antidepressants didn't do much for my mental state or change any sort of high I was getting from other drugs, but weight loss was a side effect of this medication (Wellbutrin) so it was the perfect cover.

I was also spending a good amount of time away from home. In Long Beach, I found myself involved with a crowd that was filled with trouble.

One friend of mine had an abusive boyfriend, so I helped her move out to a little hotel down the street from me. Later that night, I got a call from the boyfriend.

"I'll fucking kill you," he said. And he was serious. He had spent time in jail, and although it wasn't for murder, I didn't think he was scared of any punishment that might occur for slitting my throat. He knew where I lived. I freaked out. With my husband working long hours I was often home alone. I kept two guns in the house for safety but wasn't the type to really use one, even if necessary. Out of fear I called Shaun.

"Honey, there is this guy, he says he's going to kill me and I'm pretty sure he means it."

"Calm down. What happened?"

I told him the story.

"I'll take care of it," he said.

He had one of the other guys he worked with call the guy who threatened me. "We have a warrant out on you already," he said. "If you make one more phone call your ass will be shipped back to whatever state you came from. Trust me, we will find you."

And that was it. Shaun believed whatever bullshit story I told him and came to the rescue. That was the kind of story I would laugh about later while getting high. We all had stories like that and when we got high, it all seemed very funny. No one questioned the crazy situations we wound up in. It seemed like the crazier the story, the more normal in this crowd you were.

As much as I felt like I was pulling one over on Shaun, he knew I was hanging out with a bad crowd. He didn't like it. I knew I needed to start spending more time at home—which meant bringing my newfound meth addiction into the house.

Because there wasn't anyone around to constantly watch over me, it was pretty easy to hide. If Shaun or someone else was home, I was really good at covering it up. When you're using you're able to protect your drug use almost as you would a child. You have to—it's what's keeping you going.

I would lie about going to get my nails done and instead pick up drugs. Or I'd say I was going to the grocery store when I was really using with friends.

The friends I used with didn't look like the meth addicts you read about or see on public service announcements, so if someone came to our house, there was no clear sign it was a "bad" friend. They didn't look scary or washed out and they didn't have teeth falling out of their mouths.

One time, Monica was over and we were getting high together. Shaun was supposed to be home in half an hour and she was injecting meth into her arm in the guest bathroom. (I was deathly afraid of needles—even at the doctor's office—so I stayed away from that.) All of a sudden I heard, "Oh shit."

She had burst a vein.

There was blood everywhere.

All I could think was, "Oh fuck, my police officer husband is going to walk in and there are needles and drugs all over the counter and blood everywhere. She needs to go."

"I'm really sorry about your arm," I said. "Here's a Band-Aid. Clean your shit up and get out!"

Sensitivity goes out the window when drugs are involved.

I had everything cleaned up in time, and Shaun, once again, had no idea what had just happened.

While I stayed away from needles, after about a year of snorting meth, I switched to smoking it. My nose was so raw and painful that it seemed like the only option. Plus the people I was hanging out with were all smoking it and it seemed better that way.

Even with the pipes and other paraphernalia necessary for smoking meth, my husband was none the wiser. As long as I didn't stink of booze, I was in the clear.

He and I would get up and do stuff around the house during the day. He'd work out and I'd clean or cook and get high while I was doing it. Domesticity was my way of covering it up. I thought that if I could continue cooking and being a perfect homemaker while he was there, he would never suspect the drugs and craziness that occurred when his back was turned. After a while, it became the norm. I wasn't even really getting high anymore; I was just maintaining the addiction. When I didn't do meth I'd feel sick and sleep for twelve or fourteen hours. I needed the meth so that I could go about my everyday functions and I didn't realize how fucked up I was. I got really bold and didn't care about getting caught.

There was no stopping—not even for public appearances. In May 2004, I attended the LA premiere of *New York Minute*, a Mary-Kate and Ashley film about two girls up to high jinks in the Big Apple. I went with my husband and was high as a kite.

People who have known me a long time can see when I'm being cagey, and at the premiere, I know some of them could tell something was wrong and were shaking their heads at me—judging, disapproving. But the only people I ever got nervous around were my parents. My mom would look me in the eye and I would always come up with some excuse for what she saw. But Mom wasn't at the premiere.

The jeans I wore to that premiere were a size 24, the smallest size that Seven jeans made. The waist was even a little big on me! Now I hold up those pants and wonder how the hell I ever fit into them. Then I remember: drugs. I was virtually skin and bones. People at the premiere complimented me on my weight.

"Yes!" I thought, standing there at 102 pounds. "Finally, I look great." I felt like I finally looked like everyone else in Los Angeles. But it wasn't exactly the way I should be looking, even by Hollywood's standards.

As I walked the red carpet with my husband, totally high, I handled the reporters and their questions like a pro.

"Are you impressed with the Olsens' success?" a reporter asked. "Are you guys all really friends?"

I answered question after question, smiled for the cameras. No one knew a thing.

Inside the theater, I knew I couldn't last a New York minute without doing more meth. I had it in my purse, with a straw, in a little baggie inside a lip-gloss container. A few times during the film I snuck off to the bathroom. I had that move down to a science. Often I would do meth quickly in public bathrooms, blowing the smoke into wet paper towels so you couldn't see it. At the premiere, though, I just snorted it because I knew I couldn't bring a whole pipe. I timed my bathroom runs so it wouldn't look suspicious.

I knew it was risky, but I didn't care.

And I got away with it.

I always did.

That same month I managed to graduate with a degree in elementary education from Chapman University. I took a little longer than most since I had to retake the classes I had failed when I lived on campus. Even with my current partying ways I was able to pass classes and earn a degree.

After graduation, with plans of being a teacher one day, I took a job at a YMCA after-school program at a public school in Anaheim. I didn't have a job or anything substantial to do, so I thought this would be a useful way to spend my time and pad my résumé.

I had to take a drug test, but I got high on meth a couple of days before it anyway. Shaun knew I was taking the test. If I failed it would hurt a lot more than my job prospects. I drank lots of water and prayed to God. I passed and got the job. It was amazing.

I took it as a sign that I could continue to get away with it.

I'd party all night and then five days a week from 1:00 to 7:00 p.m. I helped kids in kindergarten through third grade. I would help with their homework, review their daily lessons, and watch them during free time on the playground. I overslept all the time and showed up late. Even worse, I brought a pipe and speed with me to school. I carried both in a case inside the red Windbreaker that I had to wear, and when the kids were on the playground, I'd go to the teachers' bathroom—a single stall that locked—and get high.

There was a part of me that wanted to do good, that wanted to still feel like a good person even though I was wasting my life away on meth. I didn't need this job. I wanted it. I wanted to help these kids, but really I needed to help myself.

My relationship with Shaun was also slipping away. He

became more of a burden—when he was around, I had to hide my addiction. It was a constant battle and I resented him for it.

I was married to meth and headed down a destructive path. It was going to end badly.

I knew that, but I didn't care.

chapter twelve

BOTTOMS UP

regardless of what happened, Shaun stood by me. Maybe he knew what was going on but just didn't want to believe it, or maybe he really didn't know. Either way, I was doing meth nearly every day, drinking uncontrollably, and ruining a perfectly good relationship.

The meth use started as part of evenings out with friends to party but morphed into sitting around for hours just getting high. More and more, it became about getting out of my own head, fighting the pain.

I still don't know what it was that I was so unhappy about. To some people it probably looked like I had it all. If I had to sit and list what was bothering me at the time, I don't think I could have done it. All I knew was that I didn't want to be me.

As time went on I became less and less careful about

getting caught. For two years, I was a police officer's wife by day and a drug addict by night. I thought I was pretty slick. At this point, I reasoned, if my family and friends haven't figured it out already, they never would.

I started smoking meth in the house . . . while Shaun was home. I would be in the office that didn't have a door and he would be in another room nearby. I would be smoking, sitting at my desk, with a window open and incense burning to mask the smoke.

I just didn't care anymore.

But there was one group I did care about—the *Full House* cast. I had always valued their opinions more than anyone else's. During the height of my addiction I took a break one night from my regular crowd of degenerates to go out with the people I loved the most.

The whole cast decided to get together for dinner at Taverna Tony, our favorite Malibu restaurant. Bob, Dave, John, Candace, Mary-Kate, Ashley—everyone was there, including Shaun. We were all laughing and most of us were drinking, having a great time together.

It was one of the first nights that I drank around them. I felt like part of the club. Finally, I was one of the adults. Of course, I was also sneaking off to the bathroom to snort meth when no one was looking, so really I was in a league of my own.

After dinner we decided to move the party to John's house. We were all drinking so Shaun was worried, but I felt like I had things under control. I always seemed to adapt to the habits of those around me. Around the cast, I wasn't going to fall off the deep end.

Leaving the restaurant, Ashley got in my car and Mary-Kate went with someone else. The paparazzi were following us so we had to split them up. It was quite a covert operation we were running.

Back at John's the party continued. He had recently split with Rebecca Romijn and was renting an amazing house in Malibu. It was everything you would imagine a Stamos bachelor pad to be: beautiful ocean view, wood floors, and gorgeous furniture inside, with a big patio for entertaining. It was a rental so it didn't have much of his personal stuff in it, but it was a great place to spend the summer.

Shaun dropped me off.

"I'm going to head home," he said, complaining about an early shift at work. "If you want, just stay here and I'll come back and pick you up tomorrow after work."

Ashley decided to stay, too.

We were all still drinking and having a good time. Mary-Kate left but Ashley and I got really, really drunk. She eventually got sick and John stepped up and took care of her. At some point, we all passed out in John's bed. It was totally platonic—nothing weird happened. We were just three drunk friends passed out in a bed overlooking the Pacific Ocean.

As the sun cracked through the windows of John's bedroom, we woke up, groggy and hungover. John got up to make breakfast burritos and Ashley and I moved our headaches out to the deck where we watched the waves crash on the shore and dolphins jump out of the water.

Shortly after breakfast was served, Bob Saget came back

over to John's, took one look at the three of us and without missing a beat said, "This is like the *Full House* episode from hell!"

That night was one of the first times that I felt like an adult around the people I most admired—I finally felt old enough to be on par with them. But it didn't do anything to help my addiction. The others went back to work, back to their regular lives. Maybe they drank again a week or so later. I don't know.

What I do know is that that party was just one very regular event for me. It wasn't a special occasion. It wasn't out of the norm. I'm sure I was out drinking and using again that night and the next night and the night after that.

The cast didn't know. They assumed I was like them. They thought I could separate a party from real-life responsibilities, but I couldn't.

I was on a downward spiral and it was only a matter of time before I was completely out of control.

Then it happened.

It started out as a regular night. It always does, doesn't it? I was out with a group of girls who didn't know that I was using. They didn't know I had a problem. In fact, this group of girls knew Shaun. They were friends and girlfriends of his friends. They knew him well. They didn't know me at all.

We went to the Laugh Factory—the same Laugh Factory where years ago I sat on a speaker flashing the two-minute warning light for Bob Saget. It was such a happy place back then.

This night, the stand-up comedy was hilarious and everyone was having a great time. At the Laugh Factory, like most comedy clubs, there is a two-drink minimum for all customers not being babysat by Bob Saget.

A couple of girls had a drink or two, but the group didn't drink like I did. Instead of just having sodas or ordering food or doing whatever else it took to cover our minimum, I drank my two cocktails and what the other girls didn't finish. They ordered, I made sure nothing went to waste and in a short time I was six drinks deep. Then, when a comedian wasn't so funny or I just got the urge, I snuck off to the bathroom and did key bumps of meth.

I was wasted. Quickly.

We left the Laugh Factory and stumbled down Sunset Boulevard. OK, I stumbled.

We landed at Miyagi's, an Asian restaurant with a bar and club upstairs. The drinking continued. As the other girls sipped their one cocktail each, I pounded drink after drink and continually found my way to the bathroom to take in as much speed as possible. I was drinking and doing drugs and then drinking more because I was on drugs, and became obliterated.

I was out of control. The girls had no idea.

When we left Miyagi's I started feeling sick. We got in the car and began driving down Sunset. We pulled off on to a side street. My world was spinning. Something was very wrong. I needed to get out of the car.

We were driving 30 mph and I decided to open the door. I told the girls I needed to get out of the car.

The driver was terrified. They pulled me back into the car and slowed to a stop. I fell out of the car onto the sidewalk. I was sick everywhere.

I just lay on the concrete. The group was freaking out. They looked through my purse and found the drugs. They panicked because they knew my husband and didn't know what was going on with me.

I was in and out of consciousness, lying there for twenty minutes. At first, they didn't call the police. I told them not to.

"I'm OK. I'm OK," I said. "Don't call the cops."

I knew once Shaun found out, everything would be over. I felt my world crumbling around me.

I kept getting sick and passing out. At one point I stopped breathing. I was lying there on the sidewalk, heartbeats away from death.

They decided they had to call an ambulance, despite my pleas. They were worried I had alcohol poisoning or even worse, was overdosing on drugs. As I drifted in and out of consciousness, they told me the police were coming.

"No, no, no!" I screamed. "Tell them I'm OK."

I felt as if I were being flushed down the drain. Everything around me was spinning out of control. I knew I'd started something I couldn't stop. Everything would come crumbling down, everything would be found out.

In the ambulance, the medics started me on an IV. I kept passing out. I had hypothermia. It was early spring and my body temperature had dropped from lying on the sidewalk. They wrapped me in big foil blankets. I was shaking, still vomiting whenever I could grab my breath.

My heart was beating irregularly. I had developed arrhythmia from the combination of drugs and alcohol. They took me to the emergency room at Cedars-Sinai Medical Center.

Darkness.

At some point at the hospital one of the girls flushed the rest of the speed down the toilet and called Shaun. When I came to, the next morning, he was there.

I couldn't look him in the eye. I couldn't talk to him. It was the most humiliating experience. I felt physically awful and so guilty.

I knew I had to tell him all that had gone on, and I knew that undoing the damage would be impossible. After Shaun realized that he'd been married to someone for almost two and a half years who was using almost the entire time and hiding it, who was living a whole other life, it would be impossible for him to go back to any kind of normal life or happy marriage.

I had prepared myself for that, which is why when he picked me up from the hospital, I knew nothing was ever going to be the same. It's hard enough to deal with a situation like this if you already know someone is using and she winds up in rehab. But when it comes as a complete surprise, you feel as if you don't know that person at all. That level of betrayal is nearly impossible to repair.

Everything was falling apart. My friends were going to

know, my parents were going to know. I didn't know what to do. As we walked down the hall of the hospital, out to the car, he asked me question after question. All I could do was stare at the ground.

I crawled into the passenger seat and started to cry. I started saying the Serenity Prayer over and over again. It just came to me and I didn't know what else to do. That prayer was the one thing I remembered from my short stint in recovery the first time around.

It was all I could remember. It was all I had.

> *God grant me the serenity to accept the things I cannot change; courage to change the things I can; and wisdom to know the difference.*

I knew I couldn't change the situation.

God grant me the serenity to accept the things I cannot change

I got home and handed the pipe and everything else I had in the house over to Shaun.

Courage to change the things I can

He stepped on the pipe, smashing it to pieces on the front yard. Shaun was so upset. He couldn't be around me.

Wisdom to know the difference

I packed a small bag and Shaun took me to my parents' house. That was the second most humiliating, awful, horrible moment—walking into their house. My parents were upset, but my mom hugged me and told me everything was going to be OK. I walked to the guest room, lay down on the bed, and cried for hours. I didn't want to talk to anybody; I didn't want to look at anybody. I couldn't.

For the next day and a half I stayed in their house, sick and hungover, coming down from all the drugs. I couldn't eat. I couldn't sleep. I was uncomfortable—sweating, feeling sick, and throwing up all the time. My hands were numb, I had awful headaches and shook uncontrollably.

A couple days went by. My husband came to the house and he and my parents sat me down. We agreed that I needed to go to rehab.

I had no other options. I had fucked everything up. My life had fallen apart. I was so scared and so lost; even with my parents and Shaun sitting by my side I felt totally alone. As we called various rehab centers to find an open bed, I sobbed inconsolably.

This is what my life had come to.

God help me.

chapter thirteen

ADOPTED HABITS

i checked into Passages, a beautiful luxury rehab facility in Malibu. I had called Betty Ford, but they didn't have any beds. As I was driving to Passages, a bed opened up at Betty Ford. We should have turned the car around. I probably would have had a better chance of getting and staying sober had I gone to a place that had more involvement with the 12-steps. Passages focused more on wellness and personal happiness as opposed to treating addiction as a disease.

I pulled up to the facility, a fifteen-thousand-square-foot mansion on a cliff overlooking the ocean, with my mom and Shaun. It was intimidating.

It was early evening when I walked in and most of the other clients—only about fifteen are permitted there at a time—were out at a meeting. A few others sat on the patio smoking cigarettes.

"I don't want you going out there," Shaun said. "I don't want you hanging out with those people and picking up another addiction."

"OK," I said, but that wasn't really my main concern.

We walked inside and the person doing the intake brought me to the library for the interview. My mom and Shaun waited outside. They asked a number of questions and I had to be honest about everything. For the first time I had to speak about it all.

"What's your drug of choice?" the intake agent asked.

"Speed," I said as my heart broke. No one had ever asked me that. Even the people I used with would say, "Do you have any stuff?" when they referred to drugs.

Speed. It sounded so ugly.

As the interview continued with question after question about my drug problem, I felt sick and tired and completely terrified.

It was the week before Easter and I knew I was going to be there for a month or so. I didn't know anyone. I was scared.

I checked myself in—a requirement unless you are a minor or a special mental-illness hold—and the agents went through all my belongings to make sure they were free of drugs and alcohol. My mom and Shaun gave me a hug. They were both crying and very upset. I was, too, but at the same time I thought this was a chance for me to be on my own and to maybe get my act together.

They brought me to my room and I met my roommate, but I wasn't quite ready for friends. I was terrified of everybody and felt out of place. I didn't go down for dinner that night. I just wanted to sleep.

But I couldn't.

I felt so alone.

I felt as if I'd just jumped off a cliff and my life was ending. My parents knew. Shaun knew. And there were no more secrets. The real me was out there and there was little to be proud of.

At any time I could have checked myself out. But I didn't. I didn't really have that option. I was desperate to get sober. But wanting it and being willing to go to any lengths to make it happen are two totally different things. Even if I left, where would I go?

I wasn't welcome at my parents' house. They were fed up with me. I couldn't go back to Shaun. I couldn't even look him in the eye. I had no place to go.

No matter how I felt, Passages was now my home.

The first two days I didn't talk to anybody. I avoided the smokers on the patio because I wanted to make Shaun happy. I didn't know where I would fit in. These other people had been there for a couple of weeks together. I was the new person, so I was the odd one out.

One of the first few days I was there, I met a guy named Jeff. Jeff had been there for a long time—six months or so. You can stay at Passages for as long as you want; really, as long as you can afford the sixty-five thousand dollars or so a month.

Jeff was sort of the patriarch of the place. Everyone knew him. He came up to me in the kitchen and we talked for a little bit while we raided the candy drawer. It was mostly white chocolate.

"No milk chocolate in here?" I asked.

He laughed.

I told him that I liked Toblerone and Hershey's and a few other types of candies. Later that afternoon I went to my room and on my bed was a huge bag of candy filled with everything that I had told Jeff I liked.

I went downstairs later that afternoon and ran into him.

"How did you like the little surprise I left for you?" he asked.

"Thank you so much," I replied sincerely.

It meant so much to me. We became really good friends from that point on. He was one of the most generous people I had ever met and I just loved and adored him, like a big brother. He was a bit older and such a teddy bear.

Eventually, he left rehab and went to Hawaii and started drinking heavily again. He spent about ten days there and someone from Passages went to go get him. When they brought him back, he looked terrible. I had never seen a living person that color. He was gray. This was a guy who was always outdoors, always tanned, and he walked in looking like a ghost. I started crying and knew things were bad. He stayed another couple of months and then decided he was ready to go home. The people at Passages would ask me how they could keep him sober. They thought since I knew him so well, I might have an idea. They were stuck and wanted to know what they could do. But I didn't have an answer.

On Thanksgiving that same year, Jeff drank himself into

a coma and died. Jeff was the first person that was there for me, that made me feel OK there, and I'll never forget him for that.

At no point in my struggle—the drugs, the cutting, the drinking and driving—was I ever trying to kill myself.

Even in the worst of times, I've always known that nothing is permanent. No feeling is permanent and as much as you think bad feelings will kill you, they won't. Knowing that kept me from becoming Jeff.

At Passages, I spent a lot of time with therapists discussing the root of my addiction. I had a lot of time to sit and think about how it all started; it was then that I realized it had begun before I was even born.

I am adopted.

It's tough to even see those words in print.

Janice and Sam, the mom and dad I often refer to, adopted me when I was nine months old. They *are* my mom and dad. They will always be my mom and dad and I will never think of them in any other way. And since they continue to stick by me regardless of all the shit I've put them through, there is no doubt that they feel the same way.

Being adopted plays a large role in both my addiction and my life. I knew from the time I was little that I was adopted. It was never something that was hidden from me. My mom always said, "You didn't grow in my belly but you grew in my heart."

At first that was good enough.

During the *Full House* years, my parents always told me not to tell anyone about being adopted. "People will look at you differently," they would say. This was before Angelina Jolie made adoption cool. This was 1982. Eyebrows would raise. People would come out of the woodwork claiming to be long-lost uncles or cousins. Questions would come up about a child actor being pushed into television by her adoptive parents.

People would talk.

For the record, I went into acting because it was something I enjoyed doing. I knew at a young age that I loved it. It wasn't like they picked me off a shelf and pushed me into show business. My parents let me follow my dream.

By the time I was around nine or ten years old, I started to want to know more. One day I was at lunch with my mom and I brought it up.

"What were they like?" I asked. "Did you know them?"

"Well, honey, you were born at USC County Medical Center," she told me, deciding to open up. "Your biological mom was in jail [long pause] for drugs. And they brought her to the hospital to give birth to you."

"And what about my dad?"

"He was also in prison and shortly after you were born he passed away."

She was putting it nicely. He was in the clink for drugs and for writing bad checks and around the time I was six months old, he was stabbed in the heart, killed in a prison riot.

When my biological mom gave birth to me, I was taken home by a woman who is Sam's daughter from a previous marriage. His kids from his first wife, Rose, had a relationship with my biological parents because Rose was my biological dad's aunt. It sort of makes my dad my uncle or something like that. It's all a bit confusing and when I think about it I hear that guy from *Deliverance* playing the banjo in my head.

But in all seriousness, this was the demon that haunted me for a long, long time. It's one of those things that causes you to question whether you really want people knowing your deep, dark secrets and family history.

At that lunch (it was a big day) my mom also told me that she and my dad adopted me when I was nine months old. Rose, who passed away recently in 2007, was taking care of me in the very beginning, but was mentally ill, so that was never a relationship that was going to work. My parents came to see me and I connected with them right away and it seemed like a perfect fit. My mom couldn't have kids and she really wanted one, so they were happy to make me a part of their family.

The adoption wasn't finalized, though, until I was nearly two years old. There was some red tape because my biological father was part American Indian. He was one quarter of I don't know what tribe, and you can't adopt out American Indian children without the tribe relinquishing their rights to them. I was a blonde-haired, blue-eyed baby, so I would have stood out like a sore thumb in the tribe anyway.

Once it was official, the whole thought of adoption was over and done with as far as my parents were concerned. After that lunch, I never talked about it with either of my parents again. I don't handle that kind of raw conversation well, so I just didn't bring it up anymore.

The only evidence I have of that other life is a photo of my biological dad in an ROTC uniform when he was around eighteen, a letter he wrote to his aunt Rose (Sam's ex-wife) and a handful of photos of me as a baby.

My birth mom, I'm told, had at least one more daughter with a different guy, so somewhere out there I have a half sibling or two and as far as I know, my birth mother is still roaming the earth somewhere.

I never met her and I never want to. My birth mother and my adoptive parents came to an agreement that she would never contact me and that was where we left it.

Being adopted would come up at random times in my life. For instance, it was always weird as a kid when I would go to the doctor and forms needed to be filled out, or when people said things like, "Oh, you have your mom's smile!" The thought of being adopted would always cross my mind as I smiled and nodded back.

I started to wonder whom I really looked like and where I really came from. But I buried those thoughts and moved on, at first. Then around twelve or thirteen years old I got that teenage angst and started questioning everything in my life. By the time I was in my midteens and drinking heavily, I began to think that my drinking somehow connected me to my biological parents. Maybe it was in my blood and for some odd reason I think I liked that thought back then. For me, it justified my behavior in a way.

In my house, I'm the only one that has an addiction problem. When I was growing up my parents never drank or did drugs. There was never even alcohol in the house. My mom would say that she couldn't have a glass of wine because it gave her a headache.

As I slowly put together the bits and pieces of my biological history of addiction, I knew that when I drank I was drinking like an addict. I knew that other kids at fourteen or fifteen years old weren't drinking the way I was drinking. All of a sudden my curiosity turned to anger.

There was this rage inside of me, but I still kept quiet. I didn't want my parents to feel as if I didn't consider them my real parents or that I was ungrateful. This big, ugly burden grew inside of me and controlled my behavior. I felt like an alien that got fucked up and dropped into another family. The more I drank, the more I thought I wasn't like my adoptive parents at all.

I was completely different.

When I went to college, and my addiction really began to take hold of me, I wanted to know more about my adoption and didn't want to keep it a secret anymore. So I spoke up—but not to my parents.

I talked to Theresa—a friend of mine who, as it turned out, was adopted, too. One night, we both got drunk and started opening up about our pasts, both of us breaking down in tears as we sat outside the dorms. We cried for hours.

"Fuck them," I yelled. "Fuck them for giving me this disease. Fuck them for making me broken like this."

They were people that I knew nothing about, but I knew that because of whatever it was that they had given me, I was like them and it was screwing up my life. I was angry with them for that. But it was like being angry with a ghost, because I was angry at something that wasn't real or tangible to me.

I always understood that addiction is passed down genetically, and I truly believe that I was born with addiction in my blood. I certainly didn't choose to have addiction issues. At Passages I realized the minute I picked up a drink, it was an obsession of the mind that I couldn't shake.

In counseling I played the blame game. I'm good at blaming other people. If other people just did what I asked them to, if other people behaved accordingly, if other people weren't x, y, and z, then I wouldn't be this way. But I have a part in everything. Every day I make choices and take action in every aspect of my life. I'm accountable. I put myself in bad situations and made certain decisions. I couldn't blame other people for that.

It was part of the whole process—looking at my mistakes and figuring out how I could move forward. At Passages, I thought I addressed and overcame those accountability issues, but in reality I just pushed them to the back of my mind. To this day, I'm still learning how to accept my mistakes and how to stop blaming other people for the circumstances of my life.

I realized in counseling that I was wasting too much of

my life thinking about the adoption. That part of my life was only nine months. In the scheme of things, it's such a short period of time. I don't even remember it, and yet I let it shape a huge part of me. I gave it too much power over me.

Today, there is still one reason why my biological history is burned on my brain: Zoie—my baby girl.

I look at my baby and pray, Please God, don't let her be affected by this. I know from my firsthand experience with drugs that I will be there for Zoie if she ever struggles with addiction. For better or for worse, I will have a certain kind of empathy for her struggle that my parents couldn't have had for mine. I pray with all my heart that she doesn't have that addiction switch inside her. I would do anything in the world to prevent her from struggling through life the way I do.

At Passages, though, it was all about me. I opened up about the root of my addiction. The problem now was figuring out how I was supposed to move forward.

chapter fourteen

MALIBU'S MOST
UNDAUNTED

as time went by in Passages I started making friends. I got a new roommate, Rachel, who I really connected with. We were Frick and Frack—sharing clothes, playing music loudly, and singing all the time. We instantly became inseparable.

She and I were good at making sure we got whatever we wanted. Once, Rachel and I were alone at equine therapy, a form of therapy where a group tries getting a horse to do a particular action using nonverbal communication. It was a lesson in problem solving and controlling emotions, but Rachel and I saw it as an opportunity for fun. We weren't allowed to ride the horses. No one was. Since it was just the two of us that showed up to class that day we figured we could bend the rules. We put on our cute pouty faces and convinced the head psychologist and the equine therapy trainer to let us ride. Of course, I took it too far and took the horse over a jump. That ended that, but it was only a matter of time before Rachel and I were at it again.

All around it was a good group of people at Passages. We had breakfast together every morning at 7:30 a.m. From there the day was filled with individual counseling and various meetings, as well as with morning meditation, time with a fitness trainer, acupuncture, and those sorts of things. Passages really focused on creating a sound mind and body. That was what I liked most about it. While getting acupuncture or a deep-tissue massage may sound more like a day at a spa than rehab, when you think of the toxins you put into your body as an addict you realize that all of those treatments really help clear you out. It seemed like an essential part of the process.

In the evenings we had free time to watch movies and hang out and bond as a group. Sometimes we would sit on the balcony together, talking until 1:00 or 2:00 a.m.

I was really excited and happy to feel like I had newfound clarity and friends. I thought my life was going to be perfect from there on out. I was on that pink cloud that people talk about where everything is great and perfect and happy.

There was a three-week period where we had an amazing group of people who clicked and who connected and supported one another. One morning we had a group session in the library and I don't remember why, but we were joking around and something triggered this huge laughter. We were laughing so hard that the owner of the facility heard us from the other end of the house through the huge wooden closed doors of both his office and the library. He came in and couldn't believe it. He had never seen such a happy group.

It's one of those moments that I look back on and think that if I could hold on to it and remember how much fun it was and how good I felt, I would channel those feelings any-time something went wrong. It was better than any drunk or drug-induced night. It was just this magical bond that we had. We didn't need to be drunk. We could have fun in so-briety.

When we went out to dinner at nice restaurants, we'd do the same thing. People looked at us and assumed we were all drunk or something.

When it came to rehab, though, there were really high highs and really low lows. Shaun came in a couple of times for marriage counseling. At one session we came to the con-clusion that we didn't think the marriage was going to work.

"She damaged this relationship too much," Shaun said. "She lied to me—the whole time. I just don't trust her and I don't think I ever will."

I couldn't dispute the truth.

I sat in silence.

He said everything that I knew and felt, but to hear him say that to me was absolutely heartbreaking. The truth hurt. I couldn't speak, but in my head I was hearing the same things over and over again.

"You ruined your life."

"You ruined other people's lives."

"What did you do?"

A big part of my using was denial. I never really thought I was that person who was lying and walking all over the people who loved me. When reality finally set it, I was devastated.

Shaun got in his car and left. I walked from the guesthouse where the therapy took place into the main house. I started to walk up the big marble staircase to my room and about three steps in I hit the ground and collapsed, crying.

My counselor, Katherine, tried to help. She listened to me in our private sessions and talked to us in the marriage counseling sessions. She helped me put things into words. She helped me open up, but it didn't matter. No matter how you say it, I fucked up.

In the beginning there was some hope that we could move forward together. He didn't like seeing me at Passages, because he didn't like it there. He was very negative about the whole place, and that was a big point of contention between us. To him, Passages was a reminder of everything gone wrong. For me this was a safe haven. This was my world. These were my friends.

When you are in rehab, you form bonds quickly because you are going through such an emotional experience together. Two weeks in rehab is like a year in the real world.

"Why do you like these people?" he asked at lunch one day with my parents. "They're all wrecks. Why do you want to hang out with them?"

"They understand me," I said. "These are my friends. They're good people."

I was talking a mile a minute, like a little girl coming

home from her first day of school. That's how excited I was about the place.

"But they're addicts and alcoholics," he argued.

"So am I, Shaun."

"Well I don't like it."

"Well I do," I said. "I love it here."

"You love it here? How could you love it? This is rehab. You're not supposed to enjoy it. It's supposed to be painful and horrible."

"I've never been happier."

"Are you on something? You're crazier now than when you were using."

He didn't get it.

Maybe there were times that I enjoyed it too much and got a little too comfortable, but for the first time in my life I had found people who thought like I did, acted like I did. I would feel, but not understand the feeling; think, but not understand the thought; act, but not understand the reason for my actions. These people understood. Shaun did not.

Looking back, Shaun had a point. To some extent it was all a joke. We called Passages "Club Rehab." We would go to The Palm or Spago in Beverly Hills for dinner, to Rodeo Drive and other high-end places to shop. We didn't have a ton of rules, we were going out with chaperones from the center called techs and living a life that I had never really lived. It was the ultimate in posh luxury and we were all recovering addicts. One trip to rehab and you're living the good life. It was like this dream world that I didn't want to leave.

Chris and Pax Prentiss, the founders of Passages, have great intentions. But when you're charging that much money for people to go to rehab and claim in your book that you have a cure for alcoholism and drug addiction, that better be the case. Almost every person I've known that has gone to rehab there has relapsed, so something's not right. That's not a cure. Even AA has a better success rate than Passages—not much better but better. The bottom line is there is no cure for alcohol and drug addiction.

Though there were plenty of absolutely heart-wrenching, falling-on-the-floor-crying moments during therapy sessions, meetings with counselors, and arguments on the phone with my parents, overall it was a comfortable lifestyle that I didn't want to leave. Who would?

The thought of going back home to normal life didn't seem so appealing. I had destroyed my real life and had no desire to go back to it. In the bubble of Passages I lived like a queen. Yes, I was sober, but it wasn't the real world. How could I go from this back to that?

My relationship with Shaun continued to deteriorate. Every time we talked it was just bad and hard and uncomfortable. I don't do bad and hard and uncomfortable very well—I usually run from it.

This time I ran right into the arms of a married man. Austin—a sandy blonde-haired, green-eyed athletic hunk with a sick sense of humor—moved into the room next door toward the end of my stay at Passages. He had the same sorts of issues and problems that I did, which was very attractive. Most of the other guys at Passages didn't have the right look or age or sexual preference that I was looking for in a companion. Austin? He would do.

I knew from the beginning that he was married. He knew I was married. We were flirty anyway. Caged in this house, sitting through therapy together, emotions began to fly. Add to that the fact that I had checked out of my marriage mentally and it was trouble in the making.

One night Austin and I were hanging out on our joint patio, gazing at the stars, talking about life and how misunderstood we were by our spouses. Sparks flew. We kissed a long, passionate kiss. My heart was racing.

Shortly afterward, we went back to our respective rooms. I was dying to tell Rachel what happened. With all the drugs I was doing before rehab, I hadn't so much as kissed Shaun in a long time. That kiss just felt nice. There was a little guilt at first but it went away quickly. I knew things with Shaun were irreparable at that point anyway, but this kiss sealed the deal for me. It made it easier to walk away—I knew that I wasn't going to be alone.

Austin and I moved our relationship forward, but it was touch and go because, well, we were both married. His wife, who actually has the same birthday as I do, came to visit one time and we all went out to dinner—probably a bad idea.

Accompanied by a tech, a small group, including Rachel and me, joined the couple at an Italian restaurant in Pacific Palisades. Everyone at the table knew what was going on between Austin and me, except his wife. She was trying to be friendly to everyone, but he was being over-the-top attentive to me and she was clearly threatened by it. You could cut the tension with a knife. The rest of us lived together, so even though she was his wife, she was the outsider.

We made it through the night, but nothing at Passages lasts forever. Eventually, Austin moved back to his hometown in Texas with his wife. I had to move on, too, but not yet. After a full month's stay I decided to add another two weeks. I wasn't quite ready to go home.

Rachel and I started talking about going together to Transitions, a sober-living facility that doesn't have inpatient treatment; it's just a fancy house in Malibu where you can live among other sober people. You make your own appointments out of the house to see therapists and counselors and whatever else you may need. It's like a 90210 version of a halfway house, and in this case, it was a home that was formerly owned by Pam Anderson and Tommy Lee.

You might have even seen the house on MTV's *Cribs*—movie room, Starbucks, and that pool where that poor kid drowned, which was always a bit creepy. But other than the pool thing, it was a pretty sweet pad. At the end of my extra two weeks, I decided to head to Transitions.

I packed up my belongings at Passages before Shaun came to pick me up and take me to my new home. At that point I was smoking cigarettes all the time. It was my new addiction. I remembered how much he hated that group on the patio when I first checked in. I remembered his warning to stay away. For me, like many addicts, the minute you tell me not to do something I want to do it even more. It's my big "fuck you" to whoever is trying to control me. No matter how bad or unhealthy it is, I'm doing it.

So when he came to pick me up to move to sober living, I was standing on the balcony of my room smoking a cigarette. I knew he was going to walk up. I knew he would see me smoking. I knew it would blow up into a huge fight. But I was looking for a fight. I knew our relationship was falling apart and instead of talking to him, I smoked my way right out of it.

This time I anticipated a big blowout, but there was nothing left to say. It wasn't worth the shouting. The day I moved to Transitions, Shaun and I decided to end our marriage.

chapter fifteen

TRANSITION IMPOSSIBLE

once i was in Transitions, I was on my own. There weren't organized meetings or therapy sessions. It was just a house filled with people like me.

Recovering alcoholic, plus freedom inside a Malibu pad that used to be owned by Pam Anderson and Tommy Lee, seems like a recipe for disaster, but once you've put in time at rehab, you're supposed to be able to function on your own. So I gave it a shot.

Rachel and I grew even closer. We had the same interests and we shared everything, including clothes since we were the same size. We went to Pilates, sat at the pool, saw movies, and even caused a little trouble together.

Once while driving home from the Third Street Promenade in Santa Monica, we were stuck in traffic after a day of shopping. In the car next to us were two attractive guys. I offered her twenty dollars to flash her breasts. Then she paid me sixty dollars to do the same. (I guess my breasts are more valuable.) The shocked looks on the guys' faces were priceless. We couldn't stop laughing and all bets were off as we drove the whole way home with our shirts on the floor. Ah, the freedom of Transitions.

From the get-go, I was single. Shaun and I were working on our own time to make it official. We had a prenuptial agreement and respected each other so even though we were upset and angry, the split was relatively easy. We figured everything out amicably without separate attorneys and with the help of a mediator that came highly recommended by John Stamos. When it came down to it, it was easier for both of us to just walk away peacefully.

I was acting single and looking to see what was out there from the day I got to Transitions. Mentally, I knew my marriage had been over since I met Austin, but I never stopped to deal with the fact that I was losing the relationship I had with Shaun—a relationship that started when I was in high school. I didn't want to feel its end. Instead of coping with the loss, I allowed my eyes to immediately wander to every cute guy in the room. It was my way of distracting myself from having to feel anything painful. I simply pretended the loss didn't happen.

Austin, while still married, came to visit me a couple of times. His wife thought he was visiting his father, who lived in Marina del Ray. When he wasn't around, my wandering eye moved to the guys inside sober living, which is a really bad idea—just ask Dr. Drew! It's sort of like fishing in a dirty pond. Stable, healthy men with their shit together don't exactly check themselves in to these kinds of facilities. Trust me, I know. I was the Michael Phelps of that dirty pond for a while.

Remember how I said that Rachel and I shared everything? Well, it turned out we also shared an interest in the same guy: Joey. He was tall, dark, intelligent, and funny, a very good-looking—part surfer, part preppy—real all-American boy. She dated him in Passages before I was there and I knew him only briefly before he moved out. When he turned up at Transitions, he and I instantly hit it off. He was the new guy and everyone loved him, but I was going to make him mine.

Whenever Rachel wasn't around, Joey and I would flirt and plot how we would make this relationship work behind her back. Eventually we thought we had it figured out.

One night after I returned from spending the day with Rachel and her family in San Diego, she and I had plans to see a movie. I told her I wasn't feeling well so she went without me. Instead of resting in bed as I had promised, I went to dinner with Joey. It was our first real date. It was a long time coming, so that date was more important than Rachel's feelings. We went to Chapter 8 Steak House in the Valley and sat outside in a cabana by the fire pit. It was very romantic. We talked for a long time, ate filet mignon and, at the end of the night, he kissed me. I knew Rachel would be mad but at the time I was too selfish to care. I was so happy that we kissed.

Of course, Rachel's movie ended before our dinner did

so when she saw that I wasn't home she was furious. The others in the house told her where we had gone, and when we got home she let me have it. There was a lot of door slamming and threats to leave. Ultimately, I spent the night on the couch in the theater room. Rachel and I were like an old married couple. We'd fight and someone would end up on the couch. She or I would sulk around the house for a while, but eventually we'd sit down and talk it out and get over it.

I didn't mind all the drama. It kept me busy. Dating in general was a distraction from those feelings of loss and grief that were bubbling under the surface. My divorce was being finalized and it was wearing on me. I needed to fill up my day even more, so I decided a job would help keep me busy.

Shortly after moving into Transitions, I started working at Passages, the rehab facility that I had called home not that long ago. I had only forty-five days of sobriety under my belt but I convinced them to let me be a tech at the facility. I was the first client they had working there that quickly—usually you had to be sober for a minimum of a year before you were handed that sort of responsibility. Maybe they wanted to keep an eye on me or maybe they really trusted me. Either way, I was living in Transitions, barely holding on to my own sobriety and helping the incoming patients at Passages. Not the brightest idea.

One of my jobs was to help move clients into the facility. On one such occasion, I was asked to move a college girl out of her dorm. She had spent time in rehab before, attempted college, and was now moving back. We had a lot in common.

She was a recovering meth addict who struggled with college life and who seemed lost in her own world.

My job was to help pack up her stuff and drive her to Passages. As we were putting her clothes, books, and shower shoes into a box we stumbled across a bag of meth that she had forgotten she left behind.

"Oh my God," she said, freaking out.

"It's OK, let's just get rid of it," I replied.

I had it in my hand and was walking back and forth to the bathroom. A part of me wanted to flush it down the toilet, but a part of me didn't. I walked back and forth to the bathroom six times. I leaned against the wall and fell down to a sitting position.

"What did you do?" she asked when she found me sitting there with the bag in my hand.

I knew I was supposed to be the responsible person. I was supposed to pack her bags and bring her to rehab. That's it. Instead, we opted to get high.

Fuck it.

She didn't talk me into it, and I didn't talk her out of it. We got high and packed; packed and got high some more. I drove us back to Malibu, dropped her off, and tried to avoid talking to anybody there. She did the same thing. Inside I walked past my old room and began tearing up. What had I done?

They questioned her and she tried to cover for me. They called me in and asked me about it. I tried to cover it up, exhibiting the usual addict behavior, and denied everything. I felt so bad, so guilty that the next day I knew I had to come clean. I was really angry at myself but I had to be honest about it.

It was my first test and I failed.

Sobriety wasn't at all what I expected.

Though it seemed like a good idea to stay busy by help-ing clients feel more comfortable, being in a situation like that was too much for me to handle. I should have just flushed the meth down the toilet. I was trying to help some-one else, when really I needed help myself.

My job at Passages ended quickly and between the other struggling housemates and the lack of rules and structure, I wasn't really sure that Transitions was the right place for me. I didn't know where else to go, so I stayed and tried to de-velop friendships and remain sober. But after all my hard work to stay clean, I wasn't quite ready to give up drugs.

I thought a real relationship was exactly what I needed, so I let things with Joey get serious. At first it was fun and excit-ing, but it was hard for me to maintain anything healthy.

He didn't make things any easier.

He was an addict and not trying as hard as I was to stay clean. For the first time I found myself on the other end of the addict relationship, and it sucked.

He would go to lunch with a friend and say he'd be back in a couple of hours; it would be two days before he'd return. Since I was trying to stay sober, I would pretend that he was, too. Even though I was just dating Joey, I still felt completely powerless. There was nothing I could do to save this guy or our relationship. I can only imagine how Shaun, who loved me so much, must have felt.

I hated that feeling of caring about somebody who would disappear for days at a time, never returning my phone calls. I never knew where he was. I knew he was somewhere using and it was terrible to deal with.

Payback is a bitch.

I had always dated guys who wanted to help me or take care of me and now I knew why I did. There wasn't room for two addicts in this relationship. I couldn't deal with someone as messed up as I was, someone who loved drugs more than he loved me. There was no way I could handle being the strong, rational caretaker. How would that benefit me?

He moved out of Transitions eventually and I was OK with that. I still had Rachel. We were as good to each other as we could be in our separate but equal illnesses. Everyone in Transitions was the same: none of us could handle relationships. Whether it was with friends, family, or lovers, we all had trouble functioning around other people. When addicts are thrown all together in a living situation, all hell breaks loose.

Rachel and I both had insecurities that we dealt with, but we tried not to let them affect our friendship. She had a really good heart and I think that's what kept us friends. Even with all the shit we went through and everything we did to each other, underneath it all we understood a lot about each other as friends.

As strong as our bond was, we were a weak duo when it

came to drugs and alcohol. In Transitions we relapsed a couple of times. One night, the whole group in the house—about five or six of us—left the house with plans to play miniature golf. Someone in the group suggested picking up cans of whipped cream to do whipits, a way to get high off the small amount of nitrous in the can.

"If we're going to do that we might as well get drunk," I told the group.

Rachel agreed.

We picked up a handle of Grey Goose and got lit. Back at the house I passed out underneath a massage table in a therapy room downstairs. Around 3:00 a.m. I woke up and attempted to stumble back to my room. Instead, I accidentally took the elevator to the owners' private quarters. Busted.

The next day I came clean to the supervisors. I was disappointed in myself, but thought it was just a hiccup in my recovery. I didn't think it was that serious.

I left Transitions in October 2005, after living there for six months, but the people that ran the facility didn't want me to move out; they were really worried. I was confident and dying to get out so I didn't listen.

I went to my parents' house for a couple of days.

"You can stay here as long as you need to," my mom said. "I think it might be best."

"Hell no," I thought. "I'm not doing this."

I took the first apartment I could find and immediately made a bad decision. I let Joey move in. It was my place but his lease was up and he didn't know where he was going to live, so I let him stay with me. My parents, my counselors at Transitions, and everyone else around me thought it was a bad idea. My married boyfriend in Texas wouldn't have been happy about it either, but I didn't tell him. I thought I knew better than everyone else. I thought I was in control of my life and the decisions I was making.

Joey was using, but I thought I was strong enough to be around it and to stay clean. After about five days of watching him do coke, I joined the party. He was in the living room and I was in my bedroom. He had a plate of coke with lines cut up on the kitchen counter. I was sitting in my bedroom and thought, "Fuck this!" I walked out, went right to the kitchen counter, and did a line. I was sick of keeping myself cooped up in my room, sick of him being high without me, and tired of the lack of communication between us. I thought getting high together would solve the problem. This situation wasn't working and instead of getting rid of Joey I thought getting high was the better option.

"What are you doing?" he asked.

"I don't know," I replied.

That first line of coke broke the seal. I kept going, taking down all the cocaine in sight.

Then I called Austin. After a brief conversation, he was so worried about me that he dropped everything and flew out to see me. The next day I picked him up from the airport and brought him to the apartment where Joey was waiting. They didn't know about each other, so obviously that didn't work out well. Both were confused to see each other and it led to a four-hour argument that ended with them realizing I had two boyfriends at once.

Austin stormed out the door with demands: "If you don't come with me it's over," he shouted.

Joey followed suit: "If you go with him it's over."

I was stuck between a cokehead and a hard place.

My solution was to go with Austin to his dad's place, then ditch him and return to Joey. When I got back to the apartment, Joey was waiting and so were the drugs. I couldn't control myself. I started with a little coke and never looked back. I did so much coke and Xanax that I didn't remember the next three or four days. When I finally came to, I apparently had been grocery shopping and had gone to PETCO. I didn't remember any of it. It was scary.

I packed a bag and headed back to Transitions. The first night back is hard to remember. I was still coming down.

Whenever I came down from a bender, I'd be depressed and really tired. Coming off meth and coke and not having eaten for days, I'd be ravenously hungry and hungover, with a massive headache. I'd also get panic attacks and feel really stressed out. It was still nothing like the violent sweating, awful vomiting, and relentless itching that you see in movies. It would probably have been easier to stay sober if I had those sorts of reactions!

I definitely did not want to be back at Transitions that first night. Joey was at the apartment trying to stop using on his own and going through bad withdrawal: freaking out, crying, and losing control. He refused to get help. And since he was still using, he wouldn't be allowed into Transitions anyway. Once I checked in, I wanted out, but I didn't have a car and the keys to the house car were hidden. One of the supervisors came down in the middle of the night as I was rifling through the cabinets. I had opened every drawer in the kitchen. I wanted to get out of there, one way or another.

Eventually I wore myself out and crashed. I slept it off and knew I had to stay. I had to turn my life around and this seemed like the only solution.

I stayed forty days.

While I was there I was going to treatment every day at a center about three miles away. The first few days, I just sat there with my arms folded.

"This is Jodie, our new client," the rep said.

"I don't want to be here," was my immediate response. "I hate this place."

I was not an angry person when I went to rehab the first time. I was sad and hurt and scared. The second time, I was angry. It's been said that with addiction, you get stuck both socially and emotionally at the age at which you start using. I was stuck at fourteen, in a rebellious teenage mind-set, and believed I didn't need anyone to help me get my life together. I thought I was fine. I thought I could take care of myself. But I didn't really want to deal with reality or ever become an adult. I wanted to abandon ship and run away.

The first time around at Passages, I did my forty days—I missed holidays and lost Jeff but I experienced moments of great joy and understanding. This time, I felt there were no moments to savor, no one in my life worth keeping.

I tried pushing everyone away. I got rid of Joey and nearly everyone else, aside from my family. I didn't want to be reminded of my life before or during rehab. I wanted to start fresh, but it wasn't easy.

I thought the old friends were the problem. I thought they were bad for me. But it wasn't them. It was me. Friends come and go, but old habits die hard.

chapter sixteen

SAVING STEPHANIE

throughout this downward spiral in and out of rehab, I rarely thought about the repercussions. Yes, I knew I was damaging my body and ruining my relationships, but I didn't really care. What I didn't take into account was that I could ruin my reputation.

Since the time *Full House* ended I had been out of the public eye and my current fall from grace went, for the most part, undocumented. I raged in college, showed up high to an Olsens' movie premiere, and even blacked out on the streets of West Hollywood without anyone beyond my friends and family knowing about it.

At the time I thought I was pretty slick, but the truth is I was extremely lucky.

During my second stint at Transitions, I got caught. *Globe* magazine came out with a story documenting my

meth addiction and my current rehabilitation process. Someone ratted me out.

Days before the story came out, it was Shaun who broke
the news. An officer he worked with had a relative at *Globe*
who told him they were working on a story. Even though we
were divorced, Shaun called my mom who immediately
warned me that the story was about to break.

I panicked.

I thought that I had gotten away without any of my problems becoming public knowledge. I was devastated and I
felt especially bad for my family. They had hoped that this
would fly under the radar and that I wouldn't have to go
through it publicly. The fact that I had made it so far without word getting out was pretty damn amazing. I thought I
was scot-free.

When I found out, I went right to my therapist.

"Oh my God, what am I going to do?" I asked her. "This
is going to destroy me. I'm so embarrassed."

"You'll be able to handle this," she said. "You have support
around you and people that love you. You'll get through it."

Globe had the basics right. The story said I was smoking
meth and had done a stint in rehab. But there were also a
number of errors, such as the name of the rehab facility and
that I had blown every penny on my addiction. There was no
doubt that it was expensive, but at that point I certainly had
enough money for more drugs. The article also talked about
some sort of *Full House* cast intervention that sent me off to
get help. It sounded sweet and very Tanner-like, but that
didn't happen. We did meet up a number of times over the

years and while I was in rehab they all took me to dinner one night, but since I was already at Passages it was hardly an intervention.

Before that now infamous dinner, Bob had called a few times to see how I was doing. He knew somehow when no one else did. Eventually he rounded up the crew and we all went out. We had a good time and laughed a lot and everyone was happy to see me working hard to get sober. They didn't sit me down and give me some big speech. As far as they knew, I was on a path to recovery and it was the beginning of good things for me. No one knew the extent of my problem, though; that was made evident by the fact they were all drinking at dinner.

"Is this OK?" Bob asked before sipping his glass of wine.

"Go ahead," I said, feigning comfort around alcohol.

They weren't going to let me drink and I think knowing that it seemed fine to them. But in my mind, I was obsessively thinking I could have that one drink then stop myself because I knew where more than that would lead me.

That was the "intervention"—hardly a textbook sit-down. Dr. Drew would not approve.

Regardless of the minor mistakes, the story was out there. I was a recovering meth addict. People frown on meth. Even coke addicts turn their red, destroyed-cartilage noses up at meth users, which, to be honest, I never really understood. To me, an addict is an addict is an addict, even if you're a cokehead trying to be a Hollywood big shot. I knew that meth was considered an awful street drug for white-trash losers, though the fact is, unfortunately, young kids everywhere are doing meth. It's not just a drug for homeless people; it's accessible to the average American and extremely popular with middle- and upper-class kids as well. But meth more than any other drug has come to symbolize failure.

And that's how I felt when the story came out—like an absolute failure.

I needed to do something.

In February 2006, two months after my second stint at Transitions ended, I was contacted about doing an interview on *Good Morning America* and also sat down with a reporter from *People* magazine and told my story. It wasn't exactly my shining moment, and I wasn't thrilled about going public with everything. I especially didn't want to be lumped into a group of child-star screwups—I couldn't believe I was going to be one of them.

But going public gave me hope that I could move on quickly. I also had this idea that my struggle may even help people. I could, as they say, turn a negative into a positive.

For that to happen my story had to be just right. It was pretty shocking, the middle child from *Full House* hopped up on meth. But to save my reputation, to return to the girl that the public once loved so much, I had to tell the story in a way that was uplifting and inspirational.

I couldn't go on national TV and tell Robin Roberts that I went to Transitions twice and relapsed a number of times and was barely thirty days sober. That's not how it's supposed to work in Hollywood. You're supposed to go to rehab once, for thirty days, and come out magically cured—that's what people want to hear.

I had to lie.

I couldn't tell my real story.

I sat down with my agent and my therapist. We tried to put a Band-Aid on my situation, put a positive spin on it. I wanted people to believe that I was doing well, to think I was OK. And a part of me hoped that if I said it, it would just come true—that maybe, just maybe, I would wake up the morning of my interview on *Good Morning America* and actually *be* OK.

My parents and my agent didn't even know about some of my relapses, so I was lying even to them. If they bought what they heard, I thought, maybe they, too, would believe in me again.

The night before the big show, I was in my New York City hotel room freaking out. I was so nervous that I couldn't sleep. I knew what I wanted to say, and what things to avoid and dodge my way around, but I wasn't 100 percent confident I could pull it off.

I convinced myself that my relapses were none of anyone's business. It was intrusive enough that my story had come out in the first place, so I decided to admit the bare minimum and keep the rest to myself.

So there I was—me and my story versus Robin Roberts and her questions.

It was like an out-of-body experience. Thoughts such as "I can't believe I'm doing this right now," "How did I get here?" and "What the hell happened to me?" were racing through my head as we talked.

I could probably have thrown up six or seven times

during those couple of minutes. I get a bit nervous on live national TV anyway, but under these circumstances it was torture.

The interview started with a *Full House* montage—middle child, adorable Olsens, yada yada yada. So far so good. Then Robin asked about rehab and how my addiction got started and I gave pretty general answers. Of course, the interview ended with Robin asking me to say, "How rude!" I can never get away from that. A two-year meth addiction and I'm still only pulling ratings with "How rude!"

Then it was over. Deep breath.

I survived. I didn't explode on national TV, or throw up, or fall out of my chair and pass out. What a relief.

Then I did my *People* magazine interview. I had to remember what I had said on *Good Morning America* and make sure that I said the same things to the magazine. I was so good that even I started believing my lies.

Plus, both *GMA* and *People* asked similar questions. When did you start using? What was the appeal of meth? And like everyone else, they were obsessed with the fact that Shaun was a cop and didn't know what was going on inside his own home.

No one grilled me on my sobriety or questioned the facts in my story. It seemed like these news outlets were happy enough I was admitting to having used meth and liked the idea of a happy ending. That worked for me. I also had an appearance scheduled on *Larry King Live* which I canceled after it was postponed a number of times. That was it. I was safe. Thank God. I came off looking pretty good for a recovering meth addict.

For the next six months I remained sober. Now that Shaun and Joey were out of the picture, rehab and sober living were a thing of the past, and I was finally on my own, I thought that maybe I could live a normal life. But, for the first time, taking care of myself was all my responsibility. I went from living with my parents to having a roommate in college, back to my parents' house, in with Shaun, then to rehab and sober living. I was now alone. I wasn't quite ready to handle that.

There was an empty space in my bed that needed to be filled. Austin left his wife, and slid right in.

At first, everything went really well. We went to recovery meetings together nearly every morning. I was taking the steps to get my life back together.

For all my hard work I landed my college-circuit speaking gigs, talking to kids around the country about my story and the dangers of meth. I knew I was playing with fire. These kids could ask just about anything during the Q & A portions and I was fearful that my real struggles would surface. But a part of me thought that giving these speeches would force me to stay sober; in order to keep the story together I would have to actually make it true. Right?

In any case, public perception, my future in acting, and, of course, the income from the speeches all became equally important. I couldn't lose any of it. I didn't have any other income so I couldn't afford to lose those speeches. Eventually, I wanted to get my career back on track.

It was hard to live up to the adult version of Stephanie Tanner that I set for myself. I knew I wasn't the girl I was talking about in the interviews or the speeches. I constantly let myself down and set myself up for failure. This time failure was right around the corner.

chapter seventeen

FRIENDS IN LOW PLACES

my sobriety as proclaimed on national TV was short-lived. I didn't care. To me there was no turning back once I started to relapse so why not just live up to the bad-girl reputation I had created for myself? Even if I got caught, I thought I would be giving the world what they expected anyway, so I pushed common sense away. That was a lot easier than actually getting my life together.

It was a slow process, falling back to the dark place I was in before. This time around, I fell lower and harder, to a bottom I didn't even know existed.

It all started with alcohol.

I had signed up for an acting class. Regardless of my addiction, at heart I always loved to act. I thought taking a class would look good on my résumé and get me back in the swing of things. It also seemed like a good way to make new friends.

Those new friends socialized by drinking. I started debating with myself.

I can drink, I thought. Everyone else does it. I'm single and young and I need to socialize. How can you do that without drinking once in a while, right? I drank probably three times what everyone else was drinking on those nights out. We would go to bars around Burbank, hang out, and drink—it seemed so innocent. But as the others picked themselves up after a night of drinking and went to work or back to their regular, sober lives, I began to find people who wanted to continue the party.

I wanted to be out. I needed to be among people. I wasn't content sitting home, doing nothing. I had too much time to think. Thinking was bad. Alcohol was good. To me, it was one or the other—developing other hobbies or interests wasn't an option.

Austin saw that I was drinking and fell right off the deep end with me. Nights among friends at dive bars turned to small house parties and, as per my usual, coke and Ecstasy.

I continued doing the speeches. There were many nights like that night at Marquette University, where I stood up there, patting myself on the back for my recovery while getting high that same night. I was supposed to be a role model for these kids, to show them that you can bounce back from a drug addiction. Instead I was a liar—a sad, depressed liar.

But I had to keep the lie going. I needed the money and I had to save face. I didn't know how I was going to keep it up, but I knew that if it came out that I was involved in drugs again, I would be considered a liability. I didn't want to be that, even though I was and knew that I was.

The lying became part of the daily grind at these college appearances. I would talk. They would listen. Everyone left happy—until someone sitting in the lecture hall would come up to me after the speech and thank me for being so honest about my story.

"Thanks for talking today," a student would say. "I have a cousin that . . ."

Or, "It's really nice to see how far you've come. You're a real inspiration."

Inspiration—that word would echo in my head as I smiled, said, "You're welcome," and fought back every tear that coated my often dilated pupils.

It was times like those that I actually hoped they'd just ask me to say "How rude!"

That's much easier.

When I would return home it was usually back to partying. I bought the house in Westchester from Austin's dad and we planned to move in together, but using was taking a toll on our relationship.

Back in Texas Austin was a lawyer but out in LA, he worked as a private investigator. Maybe it was paranoia from the drugs or maybe he hated the fact that I was making new friends, but he started using his PI tactics on me, tracking my phone calls, spying on me, and threatening to tell the world about my problems.

The weekend escrow closed on the house, I decided I didn't want to be with Austin anymore. I told him it was over, but much to my dismay, he decided to move into the house anyway. He refused to leave. Of course, he knew way more about me than I wanted the world to know at that time, so I had to handle the situation carefully.

While people with law degrees helped control the Austin situation, I lived in an apartment with Hilary, a sweet, drug-free, earthy, free spirit I met in acting class, in a living-room-turned-bedroom setup. Things were going fine until the apartment was broken into. I wasn't home but Hilary was. We had to get out of there. I did some couch hopping and eventually landed in an apartment in Burbank, back with Hilary. As I said, I wasn't quite ready to be alone.

I also had no intention to stop using drugs. I had that one night with my friend who came over to play cards—the night when I did meth again for the first time since being clean. That was the first lapse. I tried taking a step back after that night by not using again, but that effort was short-lived.

The full relapse began one night when I went to visit a friend of mine who lived in Marina del Rey. He was a guy I partied with the first time around, prerehab. I knew what I was getting myself into. I was almost positive I would fully relapse. I was actually looking forward to it. I was already drinking pretty heavily, so this was just the next step. There was a brief moment when I thought that maybe I would make the right choice when offered speed, but I was too excited to get high to turn it down.

So I did it.

There was no remorse. No guilt (yet). It was just like riding a bicycle. I was back.

I returned to my Burbank apartment that night and tried to hide being high from Hilary. All of a sudden, I felt the need to pretend. Though I wouldn't admit it then, a sinking, guilty feeling started to simmer. I knew Hilary would not approve of speed, so I'd need to keep it quiet.

Soon enough, I was staying out all night, making trips down to Marina del Rey, doing speed, and partying at local bars. My apartment in Burbank, without traffic, was thirty minutes away. It was never a trip I wanted to make.

Austin finally moved out so the house in Westchester was mine again. I had decided to sell it, but in the meantime, since Westchester was right next to Marina del Rey and even though the house was empty, it seemed like a better option for crashing.

Some nights I'd go back there and pass out on the wood floor with just my sweatshirt balled up underneath me. Or on a big night, I would pass out on the patio surrounding the fire pit in the backyard.

After a few nights of the wooden floor, I upgraded to an air mattress. Slowly but surely, I started adding furniture, one piece at a time. A couch. A TV. Eventually, Hilary moved out of the Burbank place and when the lease ran out I moved into the Westchester house full-time.

That's when things got ugly.

My addiction went full throttle. I let a friend who dealt speed move into the guesthouse attached to the back of the house. It was instant access. We would sit around and get high all the time. My other friend John moved in and he started getting high. I started collecting a ragtag group of people in the house and doing meth there became acceptable, regular behavior.

It also became acceptable outside of the house.

Unlike the first time around, I wasn't hanging out down on the beach or in dive bars around Orange County. This time I was partying under the bright lights of Hollywood. It took a little while to get adjusted to the scene. Just because you were once on a hit television show doesn't mean the velvet ropes immediately open right up.

One of my first nights out on the town, I was out with two friends I had met in rehab. We were driving around looking for fun.

"That place looks too crowded," my friend said as we passed a random bar on Sunset Boulevard.

"How about that little place?" I said, pointing to a small club. "The line doesn't look too bad. Let's go in there and have a couple of drinks."

Our party destination was a popular West Hollywood bar called Hyde, a trendy LA spot where celebrities partied all the time. There was always a big crowd outside and a small group of regulars inside. Who knew? It was next to the Laugh Factory and looked like a cool little place from the outside. So I strolled up to the door with my two friends and my 193 episodes of *Full House* and expected to walk right in. I had lots of speed in my system at that point, so the drugs added to my confidence.

Little did I know that even God would need to be "on

the list" at a place like Hyde. So me, an actress more than ten years removed from her hit show, had no chance.

We didn't get in and just as we were walking away, the bright lights of TMZ shined right in my face.

"Jodie, what happened?" shouted the man behind the camera.

It was all very funny—although it seemed slightly less funny when I saw Jamie Kennedy and Tom Green walk out of the club. Jamie Kennedy and Tom Green? What list were they on?

The next day, the story was all over the TMZ website. I couldn't believe it was a big deal. It was so lame. But I knew from that incident that Hollywood would be different. It was only a matter of time before I'd fit right in.

It didn't necessarily happen on purpose. I didn't need to go to exclusive clubs and be a part of the LA scene. But I wanted to party and I didn't like being denied access. I didn't care if it was Shaun, some other boyfriend, or the doorman at Hyde, nobody told *me* no!

I met the right people and eventually became a part of it all. I knew promoters, doormen, the party crowd, and everyone else I needed to know to have a good time—including the drug dealers.

A month or two after that night at Hyde I was out with some of the cast members from *The Hills*: Spencer Pratt, Frankie Delgado, Brody Jenner and his date, and a bunch of other people in that crew. We met at Area, a sister club to Hyde, the night before and continued the party the following night. We had dinner at KOI and then headed to the forbidden land of Hyde, the very place that had shut me out. Of course, with Brody and Frankie, we walked right in.

"I remember you," I said to the clipboard-carrying dude who had denied me entrance once upon a time. He smiled. It was a funny moment and oddly satisfying for me.

As time went on I became more of a Hollywood regular, and as I became more of a regular, I became more and more out of control. For about a year and a half, I did not have a sober moment. I used drugs day and night. As soon as I would start to come down, I would take something to make me high again. I would head off to Miami or New York or Las Vegas and not know when I was going to return. Even in Hollywood, I would pack a bag with a change of clothes, head to a club, and not know where I would end up or when I would return to my house.

Once, after a night of partying in LA, I went with a group of friends to Las Vegas on a private jet and stayed at the Wynn Las Vegas. I don't know how we pulled that off, but it was great.

We were supposed to stay just the one night so we had only the clothes on our backs. Nine days later I was still in Vegas, had spent about fifteen thousand dollars, and was out of control. One morning during that trip I woke up after having completely passed out and looked around the room. There were people walking around naked and multiple people having sex. I excused myself and locked myself in one of the bedrooms. That was a little much, even for me.

The only reason the trip came to an end was because I had to make my way to Nashville for a national speakers' conference. With practically every drug in the book in my system, I hopped on a plane (a day late) and somehow made it to Nashville. In the process I lost my credit cards and ID and had no warm clothes for the 30-degree weather in town. I wasn't in good shape and was coming off a mixture of Ecstasy, Ketamine, speed, cocaine, marijuana, Vicodin, and more alcohol than you could ever imagine.

I crashed hard.

I was supposed to speak at the conference but I just couldn't. I couldn't leave my room. I had to call the people running the event and let them know.

I called my mom in a panic. I thought I was going to die. The comedown was gut wrenching. I had to leave. My mom paid for my flight home. How I managed to physically make it through that trip is baffling. I stayed at a sober friend's house for one night to recover, but after that I wanted out. I was fiending for drugs. I walked into my Westchester house, did some speed, and felt better.

I felt like death—panic attacks, withdrawal, depression—but I felt so much better doing more drugs. After nine days bouncing around Vegas, missing my first flight to Nashville, spending a day and a half in Nashville coming down, I went home and did it all again. Just like that.

Outside of drugs, I still wanted to act. No matter what state of mind I was in, I always loved performing. I felt at home when I was on set. I continued my acting class, and while I did show up high on a number of occasions, my heart was in the right place. I was still passionate about acting.

I thought it would add to my Hollywood street cred a

bit if I could get my name out there again. In the ten-plus years since *Full House* wrapped I had only a bit part in Bob Saget's *Farce of the Penguins* and guest appearances on *Brotherly Love, Party of Five,* and *Yes, Dear* under my belt. It was maybe a week or two of work all together, and I missed performing. Part of me thought that getting back to work might force me to get my life together. But because of my mental state and, probably, my addiction, I couldn't fully commit. I wasn't doing the work to make it happen and when I'm not 100 percent committed to something, I can't do anything.

I signed on to host *Pants-Off, Dance-Off,* a striptease, music video show on Fuse TV. I was thrilled for the job but instead of using it to sober up, I just moved the party to New York where I flew every six weeks or so.

I loved the city and even thought about moving there at one point, but I was all sorts of fucked up while I was host-ing that show. It was a show where contestants stripped so most of the people watching were probably high. It seemed only right that the host be high, too, right?

I went out all night partying and never slept. Sometimes I went out with people from the show, but often I would just get high and drunk alone in my hotel room and head out by myself looking for trouble. I never had any problems finding people to party with. It was always easy making new friends when I was high.

The Olsen girls were living in New York City at the time, but we never had any contact. We may have been in the same city, but we were worlds apart. They were at NYU and

I was at Pink Elephant downing champagne, Grey Goose, and, of course, a bottle of Jack Daniel's, which I usually finished myself. It was always crazy. One time a girl chased me down the street claiming that I had stolen her coat—a Dolce & Gabbana coat that I had purchased the day before. She was yelling obscenities for all of the Meatpacking District to hear and I laughed until I'd had enough and told her off. That night, like most, ended at 6:30 a.m.

Then, two hours later, with an egg and cheese sandwich and OJ from Europa Café in hand, I showed up to work to shoot four episodes. Reeking of alcohol, I passed out in the makeup chair and when I attempted to read the cue cards I saw three of them at once. I thought I was pulling off appearing professional, and at the very least I expected my friends in the crew to keep quiet in order to keep public perception intact.

In spite of my partying I enjoyed the work. The show was the best, worst show on television—it was awful, but you couldn't stop watching. And I loved the fact that my role was the complete opposite of being Stephanie Tanner. It was more me. With the party-girl reputation I had now earned in the public eye for my previous drug use, it seemed natural for me to host a show about stripping. It probably wasn't the smartest career move but I had fun with it. A lot of people in my age group were watching and it was different from anything I had ever done before. I flew out to New York for a week or so at a time and then would stay a few extra days to party. I enjoyed myself . . . probably too much.

Whether in New York or Las Vegas, I always found the

party. In Hollywood, I *was* the party. I was a regular at Les Deux, Area, and every other club around town. I bought bottles and drugs for everyone and at 2:00 a.m., when last call would come, I would get a room at The Roosevelt Hotel and invite everyone back to my place.

I was a regular at The Roosevelt, which was a sort of black hole for me. I spent a good ten or twelve days out of every month there and knew mostly everyone, from the desk staff to the waiters at the pool to security—who on a number of occasions kicked me out for hosting too big or too loud a party. Even the cleaning staff knew me.

Once, we left the room after doing coke on the table and the straws, room keys, and credit cards used to cut the cocaine into lines were left out. While we were gone housekeeping came in and nicely lined up the straws and cleaned and stacked the keys. Now that's service.

We would party at The Roosevelt until the sun came up, sit at the pool all day, head back to the room to get high again, grab dinner, go to a club, and back to the hotel for more of the same. Nothing stopped me. If I ran out of clothes, I walked across the street and bought something from Express or the shops at the Hollywood & Highland Center. I was so afraid I would miss out on something that I wouldn't go home to get clothes. Instead I'd just spend more money.

Between drugs, alcohol at clubs, hotel rooms, and other incidentals necessary to create the party, I spent about sixty thousand dollars in a nine-month period during 2006 and 2007. But it didn't matter because I was having fun. I had a ton of friends, I was a part of the Hollywood scene, and life was stress free and surreal. I was doing coke and speed and drinking all the time, and I was completely numb to the truth. If I had stopped to think about it even for a second, I would have realized that the truth hurts.

chapter eighteen

LOST OUT THERE
AND ALL ALONE

the truth, which was buried under all the drugs I put into my body, was, of course, that this whole lifestyle was bullshit. The friends, the happiness, the confidence—all a load of crap. Without the drugs, I had nothing.

All the parties, the clubs, and the rooms at The Roosevelt—it was my way of creating a drug-induced happy place. I was buying friends. People want to hang out with you when you're the one footing the bill. It put me in a position of power and control. I felt needed and wanted by a lot of people and it seemed like I had all the right friends. When I had a table at some LA club, I'd work the phones and create the party. I felt important. Everyone knew me and I could go to all the Hollywood hot spots. I was in the "scene." I felt respected and loved and, as lame as it sounds, I felt cool.

Every now and then I even sold drugs, but I never did it

for the money. Friends would call me and I'd either hook them up or find someone who wanted larger quantities, then split it and sell half. I never made money; I just scored free drugs, which I usually shared with everyone I knew. For me, it was about the power. I liked people coming to me to get high. I liked getting that phone call from someone looking for fun.

It was a shallow, lonely existence.

I'd walk into my hotel room and often the party had already started without me. Sometimes I would be exhausted from days of partying and would pass out on the bed and the party would continue right around me. My "friends" were doing drugs, ordering room service, and drinking all the alcohol while I was passed out. I was always the girl who had a plate of blow, a never-ending supply of money, and bottles of Jack Daniel's ready. That's what they liked. But it wasn't about me at all. They didn't care about me. They just wanted to party on my credit card. With the exception of a couple of people who have since cleaned up their lives, I don't talk to any of my "friends" anymore.

I would never let myself sit and think long enough to feel lonely. I was high all the time. I had drug dealers on speed dial and would have drugs delivered to my room. If I had to wait, I had room service bring me cocktails at 9:00 a.m. If I slept, I would wake up next to a bottle and remnants of coke and before even getting out of bed I would do a line and take a shot and get my day started.

I did not let myself come down.

Ever.

There was no time to think. No time to evaluate. No time to stop and understand what I was doing to myself.

Meanwhile, I was pushing away the people that did care about me. I treated my parents horribly. My parents—who stood by me through everything—didn't know where I was or what I was doing most days. I would go to Las Vegas or New York and not talk to them for weeks at a time.

When I did pick up the phone, I was almost always lying about something. I would be in Las Vegas and tell them I was "running errands." Of course, if I was ever stuck in some terrible situation I would call them for help. They were always there for me.

But they were also telling me to get help. I would curse at them and hang up the phone.

They invited me over for holidays, but I would show up five or six hours late, or sometimes, not at all.

On Father's Day in 2006, I had agreed to go down to my parents' house and help my mom make dinner for my dad. The night before I went out and got hammered and slept until 4:30 p.m. I had gotten so trashed that I overslept by five hours and didn't even call.

By Christmas Eve, they had had enough.

I went with my mom to church then told her I was going to go home, pack a bag, and come back to spend Christmas morning with her and my dad.

"Why don't I drive with you to your house?" she asked.

I never let her come over.

"No, no, that's OK," I said, afraid of what she might see there. "I'll be back in an hour. I promise."

Instead of packing and leaving, I got high. Going to my parents' meant stopping this crazy trajectory I was on. I couldn't do it. A couple of hours later my mom called.

"Don't bother coming over," she said.

They were standing up for themselves. They needed to get on with their lives and to enjoy the holidays without me ruining things, she told me. I was ruining their lives. They were trying to detach from me because I was such a wreck, it was breaking their hearts.

I spent the holidays without my family, partying at The Roosevelt once again.

With Candace, once my matron of honor, it was the same thing. She would call me and I wouldn't return her calls.

The last thing you want when you are using and drinking is to be around people who are going to remind you of who you once were or of what you should or shouldn't be doing. Candace is a saint. She's an amazing mother, a great person, and a great friend. I couldn't talk to her. I couldn't look at her. She was just a reminder that I was a big disappointment.

Instead, I ignored her calls. She tried to help me, but I wouldn't hear it.

A bit later, *Details* magazine called my agent and said they were doing a photo shoot with former child stars.

"Would you have a problem doing the shoot with Candace?" my agent asked.

"Why would I?" I replied, shocked at the question.

I was excited about the shoot. Admittedly, I was nervous

about seeing her but it seemed like a good idea for the photo shoot. When I arrived on set, she wasn't around. I sat through hair, makeup, and wardrobe. The theme of the shoot was the '80s movie, *Heathers*, and I was dressed to kill. (Actually, I was in a short dress and hadn't been to a gym in ages so was extremely paranoid. But that's a whole different issue.) We were all ready to roll and still no Candace. I didn't even realize what was going on. I figured she had pulled out and the shoot was now just me.

Then the magazine came out and we were both in the photo together. I was shocked. It was a great picture but we never took it together. It turned out that when the people at the magazine asked my agent whether I had a problem working with Candace it was because she had expressed concerns about doing the shoot with me. I guess she thought I was angry at her since I didn't return her calls and was probably angry at my lack of communication.

Recently we got together and laughed about the whole thing. She no longer took it personally. I told her that at that point in my life I didn't return anyone's calls if that person wasn't partying the way I was partying. I pushed everyone away. Thank God she is back in my life now.

The feeling that I had lost her was devastating. But I moved on. That was how I operated. I wasn't going to let anything bring me down.

There was one other relationship that seemed to take a turn for the worse and that was my relationship with Mary-Kate and Ashley Olsen. To be fair, I can't even begin to imagine what it's like to live their lives. To be scrutinized and followed and trapped in a world of celebrity on a daily basis must be extremely difficult.

One night I ran into Mary-Kate at the opening of Pink Taco in Century City and she completely ignored me. I turned to say hello but she seemed too preoccupied to notice. Then afterward at The Roosevelt, I saw her again. I started walking toward her and she walked away.

Sometimes you're in your own world and don't want to talk to anyone. Maybe she knew what I had become and didn't want to associate with me. But I don't think that was the case. I watched her actions. I saw how she handled the situation. I was once like a sister to her, so I knew her pretty well. I don't think she was avoiding me because she felt I was a bad person. I think that, at the end of the day, she and I had a lot in common and she wasn't ready to face an old friend.

I knew that feeling all too well.

During this rough patch in my life, all my relationships were difficult—with family, friends, and especially with boyfriends.

Although I let the party crowd take advantage of me and pushed people like my parents and Candace away, when it came to guys I ran the show.

None of it was healthy.

I had money coming in from the speeches and *Pants-Off Dance-Off*. I also received five-figure checks every few months from *Full House* residuals. Money was never really an issue and I never had to trade sex for drugs. When I was using, I was buying and often paying for everyone in the room.

And no matter what the situation, guys usually did what I wanted. I didn't want a boyfriend in the traditional sense. I wanted to come and go as I pleased and didn't want anyone to stop me. I didn't want to be accountable to anyone. I couldn't really love any man, partly because I barely loved myself. I also don't think I knew what it meant to love someone romantically.

There were guys I would go out with regularly, but I made it clear that I wasn't interested in a serious relationship. Occasionally, I would date someone for a while but I inevitably screwed it up. I wouldn't get attached but would reel him in so that he'd get attached to me. Then I would bail. It was like *He's Just Not That Into You* but in reverse. Yes guys, that is possible!

I dated a guy from my acting class for a while. It was instantly an intense relationship. We were practically living together. We both drank. I was doing drugs. He knew about it, but he hated it. It was only a matter of time before it all blew up in our faces. We would get drunk and into the most ridiculous fights.

"I love you," he would shout.

"Fuck you, I love you more," I would yell back.

It hardly made sense. I would get pissed off, go out partying with friends, and come back filled with apologies. Then one day, when I didn't feel like being his girlfriend anymore, I disappeared. I pulled the plug on the relationship without a proper breakup. I didn't handle confrontation well, so instead I just packed up my stuff and moved on.

Sometimes I would be dating one guy and wind up sleeping with somebody else. Oops! I would wake up the next morning and for a brief moment, before I got loaded five minutes later, would think, "Wow, that really sucked." And then I moved on.

You can never get hurt if you hurt someone else first. I realize now that my actions were a defense mechanism. They were a way to protect myself from ever hurting. But I didn't care to deal with my own issues. I chose to bury every feeling under sex and drugs. I did whatever I wanted and didn't care who I hurt. Sometimes I wanted a guy who would party with me and sometimes I wanted a guy who would try to sober me up. Sometimes I actually thought getting sober was a good idea and sometimes I liked the idea of fighting for my right to party. Sometimes I just wanted to get laid.

I dated a guy who was more of a "friend with benefits." When I was done with him, I started dating his best friend, Mike. It got serious for a while and I took him to Coachella, a big music and arts festival in Indio, outside of Palm Springs. I rented a five-thousand-square-foot house out in the desert and invited thirty or forty people to stay with us. It was a total party house.

I never made it to the actual festival. I just partied until I couldn't see straight and then went back to LA for more.

It was too much for my body to handle and back at The Roosevelt I started feeling extremely ill. In the middle of the night I went into the bathtub, shaking and shivering with a

103-degree temperature. I also had a huge welt under my arm.

Mike—who was now my boyfriend—didn't know what to do. I went to the emergency room and found out I had a staph infection. He stayed at my house that weekend to take care of me. Three days later, I was back in the emergency room where the doctors had to cut this thing open. I have a scar under my arm now (which Internet bloggers incorrectly say was from a bad boob job) and it was a nasty experience.

Mike was right by my side the whole time. He was so caring, so nice.

Do you know what I did to return the favor? I put gauze on my wound and went back to getting high without him. Had I waited any longer to take action, the infection could have gone into my bloodstream and killed me. Mike was there to help, but I didn't let that affect me. Shortly after, I went to Vegas and forgot all about him. That was how my brain worked. I loved him for being there for me and then hated the fact that I needed him. So I got rid of him.

With other guys I'd agree to dinner or the movies then not show up. Maybe I would call three hours later or maybe I wouldn't call at all. I was a selfish bitch and an emotional wreck. I would start crying and a boyfriend would want to take care of me. Then I would yell at him to get off my ass. It was a terrible back and forth. Nothing was ever right.

The answer, as always: more drugs.

I was afraid that if I stopped running long enough to actually care about someone else, I'd have to own up to the decisions I was making. I would have to think about what I was doing and be inside my own head. So, I kept running. There was no thinking allowed. I fought it at all costs.

As much as I acted like I didn't care about relationships—having sex just for the fun of it—I was still a girl inside and I still had feelings. I hated myself for the way I treated people. I hated the person I had become. The guilt for treating guys badly and acting destructively took a toll on me mentally. At all times I was moments away from a breakdown. But, I didn't see a way out. I didn't see an end to the madness. I was spiraling out of control but there didn't seem to be a bottom for me to hit.

I had one friend, a girl who was in recovery, who tried to help me. She talked to my mom and tried to get an intervention together. I was in New York taping the show and she was going to pick me up from the airport and take me to rehab somewhere. She and my mom had it all planned out. But I found out and stayed in New York for nearly a month, until I could get home without them intercepting me.

I held myself hostage in Manhattan until they called off the dogs. They weren't going to bring me down. No one was. This was my fucking party. This was my life and I was determined to screw it up beyond repair.

chapter nineteen

VEGAS, BABY!

my life as an addict seemed to always revolve around holidays. I spent Easter in rehab, lost a dear friend on Thanksgiving, had my parents uninvite me to Christmas, and now I was about to change my life on Memorial Day. It's not exactly a Hallmark holiday, but when you are in the party scene, all long-weekend holidays are excuses to do lots of drugs. As if I needed that. Fully loaded I headed to Las Vegas on Memorial Day 2007, to celebrate, and I left Mike of the staph infection behind.

I was basically single and looking to have a good time. As usual I was totally out of control from the second I got there. With E and coke in my system, I went with a group of friends to the Planet Hollywood Resort & Casino on The Strip. Inside one of their clubs, the party was going full force. We had an entire VIP section to ourselves and I put on a show for everyone, swinging around a stripper pole and dancing wildly to various rock and hip-hop songs. The room was spinning. I was the center of attention, handing out Ecstasy to whoever wanted some, and grinding on that pole like a pro.

We hit another club and then about a dozen of us went back to my friend's house, where the party continued. Night turned to day and we were eating breakfast the next morning while continuing to put whatever was left of the drugs and alcohol into our bodies. At around 9:30 a.m. two guys came to the house—Kevin and his friend Cody Herpin.

"Can I get you a drink?" I asked Cody, immediately thinking he was kind of cute.

At first he completely ignored me so I poured a glass of Jack Daniel's for myself. Little did I know that that was his favorite drink.

"OK, sure, why not," he said, deciding to join the party.

Cheers.

So we sat and drank and then a smaller group of us moved the party to Kevin's house. He had a pool.

We spent the whole day there. People were doing lines of coke, drinking heavily, and partying like college kids on spring break.

Neither Cody nor I was looking for a relationship. Cody wasn't a "relationship guy" and as I've mentioned, I wasn't exactly sharp in the commitment department either. I did have Mike waiting back in LA, but by now he had probably gotten the hint that it was over.

Nonetheless, we really connected. That night we went out. I was doing Ecstasy but he didn't know. He was just drinking. Though there was a world of people dancing, partying, and having a great time around us, for me, it was just the two of us. We were in our own little world.

By my third night in Las Vegas, Cody and I were inseparable. I had been up three days straight plus two in LA before the trip so I was exhausted. Instead of going out, we curled up on the bed and ordered room service at the hotel room I had gotten for the remainder of my trip. I didn't want to be with anyone else. I didn't care about missing the fun. When I had the staph infection, I was so angry that I was missing the party that I slapped on a Band-Aid and went out. Now, none of that mattered. Cody and I just wanted to be together. Alone.

The following night—my last in Vegas—we went out for sushi. It was like a real date—an actual boy and girl dinner date. I didn't flake out. I didn't call with some excuse. We went out on a date and I had a great time. He even bought me a present. He loved pigs for some reason and a kiosk in one of the hotels was selling necklaces with pig charms. He surprised me with one of those all wrapped up. It was really sweet.

We drove separately back to LA, and when I got home I realized that I had lost my phone for what seemed like the seventh time in the past year. Worse than losing the phone was the fact that I had lost Cody's number. I couldn't call him and he had no way to contact me. I freaked out at first but then through a number of connections I got his number.

We sent text messages back and forth and decided to meet up again.

That first weekend together in LA, Cody and I partied hard. We went to the club Area and photos taken of us there managed to work their way all over the Internet. I think I'm giving him a lap dance and grinding against him on a couch. I did a lot of drugs that night. The photos prove that.

I had a room at The Roosevelt and as usual the night's party was going to continue there. The promoter from Area asked me the plan.

"Tell everyone to come to my room," I told him, expecting ten to fifteen people or so.

I gave him a key and when Cody and I arrived, a crowd was already there. Lines of coke were laid out; huge bottles of Jack Daniel's were on the table. It's a party.

It started small, but people kept knocking on the door. Eventually about thirty-five people packed into the small room. Music was blasting from an iPod player that someone had brought. We emptied out the minibar, sucking down every last drop of alcohol.

I was drunk.

"How long before security kicks us out?" I shouted.

Five minutes later, there was a knock at the door.

I made as many people as possible lean up against a wall so they wouldn't be visible from the doorway. It didn't work. Security walked in and saw the crowd.

"Everybody out," he said.

Half the group left and I promised the officer that I

was working on clearing everyone else out. We kept partying.

Security came back. We all left. Cody and I walked out to ensure that everyone else would leave. We sat at the pool for a while and then returned to the room to have a couple more drinks. He eventually passed out while I stayed up, wired from all the coke I had done that night.

Once Cody was asleep I left to go visit a friend who had a bungalow by the pool. I walked out of my room and ten people were lined up outside my door waiting to come into the party. It was insane. People were just waiting for my door to open so they could come in and get fucked up. It was like some all-night cocaine store.

These people were everywhere but I didn't want them anymore. At one point during the night I looked around my room and felt like I no longer belonged. All of a sudden, it wasn't a party I wanted to be at.

I don't know exactly what was different about Cody. Maybe the timing was right or maybe we just connected in a way that I had never connected with anyone before. Either way, it worked.

He stayed with me at The Roosevelt that weekend and then we decided that he would stay at my house. (Of course, I didn't realize at that point that he was living with his mom and just didn't have a place of his own to live . . . but let's not ruin this story just yet.)

He soon moved in and helped clean up the crap that was my life. My house was a mess. He fixed it. All of a sudden, I was motivated to get my act together. Instead of going out, I wanted to stay home and cook dinner with him. If we ever did go out with a group of people, I only wanted to be near him. We just clicked.

He didn't get in my face about the drugs. I was slowing down, but all on my own. I was trying to quit doing speed. I was still doing coke and E and drinking a lot, but he was a good influence on me. It was a sort of middle ground: He wasn't Shaun and he wasn't Joey. With him, it was a happy medium.

I was starting to live a normal life. Things were comfortable and I was actually happy. I couldn't believe it. I was finally able to take a step back and look at the life I'd been living and see that it was not the life that I wanted. I wanted more and Cody seemed like the guy to help make that happen.

My friend Stefan, who was with me in Las Vegas when I met Cody, said we were the world's two biggest partyers and that this relationship was going to be a disaster. I didn't listen. I didn't want to believe him. I had found a new way of life and I liked it.

Less than two months after we met, on July 14, 2007, Cody and I went back to Las Vegas. This time, it was to get married. It seemed, with how connected we were, that once again marriage was the next logical step and I wanted to prove Stefan and everyone else who said it wouldn't work wrong. This was going to last.

It all started when friends of ours were going to Vegas to get married and asked us to come. Somewhere during that conversation, one of them said, "Hey, you guys should get married, too." They were joking, but we looked at each other and said, "Well . . . OK."

On the whole way there we went back and forth.

"Should we really do this?"

"I think we should do this. Do you think we should do this?"

"We should do this right?"

We got a flat tire. I thought, "Oh my God, what if this is a sign? Should we not do this? Maybe we shouldn't do this."

We did it.

We got the rings and I got a dress. We told a few friends and he told his mom. I didn't tell my parents. They assumed I was still dating losers so it seemed like a better idea not to tell them.

We actually looked up "how to get married in Vegas" on the Internet and realized that even here, we needed a marriage license. We went down to the courthouse around 2:30 p.m. to pick it up, and at that point we realized we wanted only us at the wedding. We wanted it to be dead-ass sober. Some of our friends were crazy, so it seemed like a good idea to leave them out.

Friends were calling and asking where the ceremony was going to be held. People were pulling into town and wanted to join us. We wanted it to be private. The Little Church of the West Wedding Chapel had an 8:00 p.m. opening but for us, that wasn't good enough. Luckily, they called back and said they could take us in half an hour. We left the courthouse, raced back to our condo across from The Strip, put on our still-wrinkled attire, and ran to the chapel.

Cody wanted a midget Elvis to perform the ceremony,

but that wasn't happening. I didn't care how crazy this whole thing seemed, I was not going there.

It wasn't exactly the huge wedding I had the first time around, but it was nice. I was excited and filled with joy. We went inside the tiny chapel after taking photos and walked down the aisle in front of Cody's best friend, Josh, Josh's girl-friend, and Lance, Cody's best man (we needed witnesses).

It was a whirlwind of emotions, but we were both really happy. I cried like a baby during the entire ceremony. Cody would tell me to stop crying, I would tell him to stop laugh-ing, then we would both lose it. But we did it!

Afterward we went out, but only that one night. The rest of the time we were in Vegas we stayed together inside the condo. It was pretty romantic for a Las Vegas wedding and there wasn't one Elvis involved.

On that trip, I did do a little bit of cocaine and Ecstasy. By most people's accounts, I was still partying heavily but for me I was slowing way down.

That would be the least of my worries.

Back in LA, a group of us were still celebrating the mar-riage with a mix of drugs and alcohol when the phone rang. I got this bad feeling in the pit of my stomach. I knew exactly who it was and I felt terrible.

"Hi, Mom."

I had called her on the way home from Vegas but got nervous and didn't tell her I got married. Coincidentally, my parents were on a trip and had come through Vegas, but luckily we didn't run into them. By the time she called me, though, word had spread.

"What did you do?" she yelled.

"What do you mean?" I said. I knew what she meant.

"Your agent keeps calling, telling me she is getting phone calls from reporters asking if you got married in Vegas," she said, extremely pissed off. "Do you know how it feels getting phone calls asking if I knew my daughter got married and I don't know the answer?"

I started crying.

"I'm really sorry, Mom."

Running off to Vegas wasn't cool of me. I never understood those crazy people who eloped in Vegas without telling anybody and now I was one of them. But during my first wedding I walked down the aisle thinking, "This isn't going to work" followed by "Oh shit, it's a little late now." This time I did it for me and I was really happy. I should have called my parents.

They had never met Cody, but it didn't matter.

"This is just one more thing you've been completely selfish about," my mom said.

I could hear my dad in the background.

"No she didn't, she couldn't be that fucking stupid," he chimed in from across the room.

"Yes, she is."

I felt ashamed.

I was really trying to get my life together and in a weird, twisted way I thought that this was a step in the right direction. Looking at it from the outside, it was just another crazy thing I had done.

I hung up the phone and did a few lines of coke. That would take the edge off. As much as I was ready to slow down, I couldn't quite stop.

It was another three weeks or so before Cody met my parents. He was freaking out. He didn't want them to see all his tattoos and immediately judge him. It was hot in August and he was going to wear a long-sleeve shirt. I told him not to worry and just prepared them for the tattoos.

We had dinner with them and it went fairly well. We had a nice time. I guess it would have been a lot nicer and easier if I had introduced them to Cody before we got married.

It was a good thing they met because a couple of weeks after that, our lives took another turn.

One day Cody and I were at home talking about our future together—whether we would have kids and where we would live.

"You should take a pregnancy test," he said to me knowing technically it was possible.

"What?" I responded. "Are you crazy? Why would I do that?"

We laughed and just to humor him I took a pregnancy test. It seemed like a funny thing to do. But then I saw the two lines and realized that I was actually pregnant. I could feel my heart in my throat. I told Cody and he turned white as a ghost. We were both shocked. We lay in bed and didn't say a word. We were literally speechless.

When we came to grips with reality I made a trip to the

doctor's office. She said that I had gotten pregnant the weekend we were in Las Vegas and all I could think about was the amount of drugs I had put into my body since then. I felt so guilty. The doctor assured me that some women go the first three months without knowing they are pregnant and drink during that time. But, uh, Doc, what about cocaine? She said I was lucky and that everything seemed fine. I still felt terrible.

There was never a doubt in my mind that I was going to keep this baby and be the absolute best mom that I could be. From day one, nothing else was an option.

This was a sign that it was time to change my life. This was my chance to turn everything around. I knew it was time for me to move on from the partying and to grow up, to be a woman who had responsibilities and priorities. I was going to make this happen no matter what it took. There were no other options for me. I'm a strong believer that there are no accidents and that nothing in life is a mistake. This happened for a reason, and I believe it saved my life.

chapter twenty

NINE MONTHS

now that I was pregnant, the plan was to act as if I knew what I was doing. I told *People* magazine that I had married "my best friend" and that Cody was an "unbelievable person," so I convinced myself that was true and planned to create the perfect family.

I was wrapped up in the idea of love and believed everything was wonderful. Because I don't do relationships well—friends, romantic, or otherwise—I defined a best friend simply as someone you hang out with all the time. Cody and I were together all the time, had fun, and hadn't killed each other yet, so it seemed right to call him my best friend.

I knew it didn't look good on paper: six weeks, married and pregnant. I wanted everyone to believe that it was OK. More important, *I* wanted to believe it was OK, and at the time I did. I kept thinking, "Why isn't everyone happy for me? Why doesn't everyone think this is a great idea? It *is* a great idea!" I wanted people to see it my way. I was determined to prove the naysayers wrong. This time would be different.

The first step was a change in scenery. I sold the house in Westchester—the house that provided the backdrop for so many terrible nights—and moved with Cody to Corona, about sixty miles away from danger. In LA traffic, that's nearly a three-day drive. We bought furniture for the house, built the nursery, and tried to make our home into the perfect place to raise a child. If the setting was right, maybe the stars of the show could put on a good enough performance to fool everyone into thinking they'd be normal parents.

The more flawless I could make the new life look and feel, the less attractive the old life would be. I knew that the old life was not healthy and not where I wanted to be, but at the same time it was comfortable. It was all I knew. With plans to change everything, I created new rules and circumstances for myself. I tried to figure out what a sober, responsible life should look like. I wanted desperately to be a good mother.

The first few months were overwhelming and confusing. The "Oh my God what have we done" thought ran through my mind countless times. I had no idea what to do. Luckily it was a really easy pregnancy. I wasn't sick and didn't feel bad, but I was tired, slept all the time, and ate a lot of Taco Bell.

My life had gone from one extreme to the other. But for me, doing drugs and partying in Hollywood was now a thing of the past.

I was going to stay sober. I had to. The second I found out I was pregnant, it wasn't about me anymore. I wasn't going to meetings and wasn't in a program, but at least I wasn't in contact with anyone who might be a bad influence. That made it a lot easier.

Just to be sure, I deleted those people from my phone and stopped answering their calls. I cut myself off from that world. No one who knew me expected me to make this change in my life. Hell, I barely expected it myself. Suddenly it was time to grow up. No more fucking around.

I didn't change my phone number (partly because it had a nice ring to it and partly because I didn't want to deal with the hassle) so the people I had partied with still had a way to reach me. The phone would ring at 4:00 or 5:00 a.m., sometimes over and over again. People would leave messages saying "Hey, this is so-and-so from New York"—or Miami or Las Vegas or wherever—"and I'm looking to get some stuff. Do you know who has any?"

Not long ago, I would have known exactly who had drugs. I rarely went out without drugs on me and at the very least, I was always just one phone call away from them. But things were different now.

After I had stopped returning calls for a couple of months, the phone stopped ringing. When you stop calling the people who live that lifestyle back, they forget about you pretty quickly. Friendship isn't exactly anyone's top priority.

Cutting off that crowd and moving out of town was a good thing because it felt like we were living a completely different life. But at the same time, Cody and I were caged in. The two of us were at the house all day together. Neither one of us had a job. Tensions started to build and I began realizing that I didn't know Cody that well.

Little things got in our way, like the fact he couldn't fall asleep without the television on. We didn't have a TV in our bedroom so even in the beginning of our relationship Cody would fall asleep on the living-room couch and I would wind up going to sleep alone in the bedroom. I started to think, "Who is this guy?" Pregnancy hormones didn't help.

We hadn't had a long relationship and most of the attraction was initially built on drugs and alcohol. During the nine months I was pregnant, we learned a lot about each other—and it only pushed us apart.

A big issue for us was money. I put all the money from the Westchester house into the new house in Corona. Now that I was pregnant, I was no longer doing speeches and after having partied and rehabbed my money away, we were really short on cash.

For the first month after finding out I was pregnant, Cody worked transportation on a Val Kilmer film called *American Cowslip*. After that he didn't work. I hoped he would take it upon himself to find a job. I didn't have health insurance and knew the hospital costs for the birth would be a big expense. It was an abrupt change of pace going from having money and partying all the time to staying in, pregnant and broke; I wanted him to do something to make things better.

We prepared for parenthood as best we could. We built the nursery and I read tons of books. I wanted to be ready.

We signed up for Lamaze classes but never went; Cody wasn't really into the idea. He tried to be helpful during the pregnancy, but I don't think he knew what to do. He never went to any of my doctor's appointments; he just wasn't interested in being there for those moments, and he'd always complain about the traffic. There were times when I needed more, but I didn't ask for his help as much as I should have. That just wasn't my style.

Sadly, on the other hand, he had no trouble asking me for things. When I was five months pregnant he asked me to get up on a ladder and help paint the house. I thought that he just didn't know any better.

I needed more support from Cody: I needed a better friend, a more supportive partner—someone who would give me backrubs when I needed them.

Being pregnant was hard enough. To top it off, I felt totally alone. I felt like Jennifer Aniston's character in the movie *The Break-Up* when she says, "I want you to *want* to do the dishes." I didn't want to order him around. I wanted him to do things because he wanted to do them.

He never did.

While my relationship with Cody seemed shaky at best,

the pregnancy proved to be a bonding experience for my parents and me. Telling my mom that I was pregnant went better than I had imagined. She took one look at me and knew. I had put on a little weight and looked healthy for the first time in a long time. She was extremely happy.

I instantly reconnected with both of my parents. Family took on a whole new meaning. My mom would call every day to see how I was doing and take me to lunch. For the first time in a really long time we were mother and daughter again. It hadn't been like that since my first marriage, since the last time I was really sober.

I finally felt like an adult around my parents. I was friends with them in a way that I hadn't been in the past, and I was able to understand them a little better. I grew up overnight.

I didn't have any close friends who had gone through pregnancy so I turned to my mom for guidance. I was scared, but she helped turn the fear into excitement. After looking at baby furniture and talking to my mom about the pregnancy, I got over my fears of motherhood.

My dad is a man of few words, but he, too, was pleased with where my life was now going, and our relationship was stronger than ever. Both of my parents could have easily pushed me away and never looked back. I guess that's what being a parent is all about. No matter what a child does, parents are always there. I love mine so much for that.

* * *

As my due date crept closer, my emotions started to get the best of me. Maybe I was going through withdrawal or maybe my hormones were taking over. Either way, I was tipping the scales at around 170 pounds and was not a happy camper.

Normally, in that state of mind I would run right to the bottle. I would be lying if I said that the temptation wasn't there. I would think of the nights at The Roosevelt and miss them a little. It was an odd feeling to have picked up and moved away from the scene overnight. But it wasn't about me now. It was about the baby inside of me and what was best for her.

Through all of this, I was trying to be as upbeat as possible but it wasn't easy. I didn't know how to take care of myself and soon I'd be taking care of someone else. With a husband bringing little to the table, I was setting myself up for taking care of two people.

The first eight months were a struggle, but by the final month of my pregnancy, I felt ready. Maybe that's why you stay pregnant for so long—it's exactly enough time to mentally prepare for the reality of what is happening in your life.

By the end, I was confident and more comfortable in my own skin than I had ever been before. Eight months away from the scene and the people who live it changed me as a person. Those crazy nights at The Roosevelt weren't even that long ago but it felt like a lifetime had passed by. You can see the change in me by looking at my photo albums on

Facebook. The headlines were More Pics, Bitches and The Debauchery That Is My Life and then Wow, How Things Change. It's drunken craziness one photo and future mom the next.

It was a complete turnaround, but I was finally comfortable with it. Even Cody and I were on the same page. We both stopped and realized what was important to us, and resolved that we would work as a team to make it happen.

Everything was in place for the big day—not to mention that I had dodged morning sickness, swelling, odd cravings, and everything else that usually goes along with pregnancy—so I was thrilled and ready.

Unfortunately, the baby wasn't on the same schedule. She was due April 5 and by April 10 nothing had happened. I was huge and uncomfortable. I thought, "OK, I'm done, you're cooked, come on out!"

I went to the hospital to have some tests done. They found that the baby had outgrown the amniotic fluid. The doctors said they couldn't let me go home and that I had to stay in the hospital. "Call your husband and family," they said. "You'll probably have the baby by the end of tonight."

"This is great!" I said. "Let's get this party started!"

Cody and his mom came to the hospital. He was in total shock. The day was here, and he, like many fathers, was nervous and pale. My parents came to the hospital as well and we were all antsy waiting for it to happen.

The baby didn't get the memo that it was time.

I was in a hospital gown, hooked up to the IV, and waiting. At about 8:00 p.m. the doctor came in to start labor but the baby hadn't dropped and I wasn't dilated.

Fast-forward thirty hours and I'm still lying there. I wasn't allowed to eat and I was starving. There were food commercials nonstop on the TV and I would have done anything for just one bite of the food they were selling.

I couldn't sit there any longer.

"Cody, will you go for a walk with me?" I asked. "The doctor thinks it might help induce labor."

"Babe, I don't feel like it," he responded. "I sat in this uncomfortable chair all night and I barely slept."

Are your eyes rolling the way mine did? There is no response to that sort of thing when you are trying to give birth.

My mom came to accompany me on the walk and Cody had the nerve to express *his* discomfort to her. "The chairs! They're terrible!"

Get over it, Buddy.

Eventually the walk paid off. I started having contractions. Finally!

I didn't want an epidural but I was in so much pain that I had no choice. I started itching uncontrollably, so they also gave me Benadryl through my IV. All the medication knocked me out. I slept for seven hours.

I woke up dilated but the baby still hadn't dropped. I pushed for about two hours. Nothing. "Somebody kill me, please!" I thought. My epidural was wearing off. I wanted someone to just take the IV and strangle me with it. Somebody. Anybody. Put me out of my misery.

By the time the doctors decided to do an emergency C-section, my epidural was out. It would be another twenty-five minutes or so before I'd be numb to the pain. It felt like a lifetime. The pain was so intense I was screaming, frightening the hell out of everyone in shouting distance.

They finally rolled me into the OR. It was game time and Cody choked under the pressure.

"I can't do it," he said. "I can't go in there."

I was angry and sweaty and didn't know how to respond.

"I can't watch," he said seeing the confusion on my face. "I think I'm going to be sick."

My mom came in with me and at 3:20 p.m. on April 12, 2008, little Zoie Laurelmae Herpin was born—8 pounds 7 ounces 21 inches long—and as healthy as could be.

I went into recovery and later that night had to go back into the ER. I was bleeding uncontrollably. But despite everything—the long, hard two days of labor and excruciating pain—I knew it was well worth it the moment I laid eyes on Zoie.

She was the most beautiful baby I had ever seen in my life.

"I have no idea what to do other than love you with all my heart," I told Zoie when I held her in my arms. I was happy and so proud to be a mother.

I lay there and fed her, hoping I was doing it right, but not entirely sure.

I had no clue where my life was going to go from that point. I couldn't imagine what was supposed to happen next.

All I knew was that I had created this precious little person and would do anything to protect her and ensure her happiness and health. No matter what, we were in this together. I would do whatever it took to be a good mother. No matter what she might do, what crossroads she might come to in life, I would always be there for her.

chapter twenty-one

THE PURSUIT
OF HAPPINESS

settling in to our new life was a bit *unsettling* at first. Everything was new and we were learning day by day how to be the kind of parents we wanted to be.

When we first brought Zoie home, she was a great sleeper, which was helpful for both of us. But during the day, the baby was 100 percent my responsibility. I was feeding her, changing diapers, and doing whatever I could to keep her entertained and happy, all while recovering from a C-section. Cody, meanwhile, played video games.

Once, after a hard day, he got off the couch and made a vegetable stir-fry for dinner. I was pretty happy. It was a nice, relaxing meal.

"This was great, Cody," I told him. "Can you take the garbage out?"

"But I just made dinner."

"So?" I said, confused. "I watched the baby all day. I changed her, fed her. I've been running around this house all day."

"But you're just better at that stuff than I am. That's why I cooked dinner."

He wanted a pat on the back for everything. He was like a child doing a cartwheel, begging his mother to watch. I cooked dinner. Did you see? I cooked dinner. See what I did? Dinner. Dinner. Dinner. Congratulations, Buddy, you made dinner.

It was always a score sheet for him. He always wanted something in return. All I wanted was to be able to sit for two minutes. On top of the grind of taking care of Zoie, I was still in a lot of pain from the C-section. Cody enjoyed that and would try to make me laugh because he knew it hurt when I laughed. That and video games were his two forms of entertainment.

Keeping up his video-game habit, though, wasn't cheap and we had no money for anything extra.

When I met Cody I was living on the money from the college speeches and *Full House* residual checks. Every penny was spent—paycheck to paycheck—on living, partying, and other wasteful expenses. Nothing was saved.

Summer break hit and the speeches stopped; the residual checks slowed and pregnancy prohibited me from doing much else. By the time Zoie was born, we were broke.

We were behind in bills so every penny we could scrape together was used to keep us from falling further behind. I didn't have health insurance anymore because I couldn't afford it and Cody didn't either. When twenty-five thousand dollars in medical bills came in, the hole grew deeper. I didn't even go to my post C-section checkup because I didn't want to pay for it. Most of the time we just shoved the bills into a drawer so that we wouldn't have to look at them, but any time money came in, we would use it to pay off debt.

People magazine approached us to do an interview and photo shoot with Zoie to reveal the first baby photos that readers love. I couldn't send out birth announcements because the photos in the magazine had to be the first ones out there, but I was OK with that; there was a little money involved, we needed it, and I thought it was a win-win situation. Cody was *really* into it, though. That was how he wanted to make money. Forget jobs. This was his answer. When the article came out and the headline read "From Meth Addict to Mom," I knew I had sold out.

It left a bad taste in my mouth. I wasn't upset at the magazine. I understand what kind of story sells. I was angry at myself for going along with it and for putting Zoie on display like that.

Cody loved it. When that (or any money for that matter) came in, he wanted to spend it in all the wrong ways. I walked in on him one day looking online at Cadillac Escalades—an impractical, gas-guzzling car.

"We can't afford the car that we have now," I said when he tried to make a case for an Escalade.

"Yeah, but when you pull up somewhere you need to make an impression," he chimed in.

"What impression will we make? That we have two expensive cars and we can't afford either one of them? That we have to park them both in our garage so they don't get repossessed?"

I just didn't understand his mentality that everything had to look good on the outside while we were broke and falling apart at home. For him, it was all about selling our personal lives and my bit of celebrity to gain status and ridiculous, unnecessary possessions.

His next moneymaking scheme was to do a reality show. I went along with it. I saw how successful Tori Spelling was with her and Dean McDermott's show and thought it could be a good move. But the more I thought about it, the more uncomfortable I became with the idea. I was really concerned about putting our family life out there. The more Cody thought about it and the closer it came to fruition, the more excited he became.

When I questioned his intentions, he would argue that he was trying to help my career, but it sounded more like he wanted to be a star in his own right. Whenever we went to events, he always wanted to be in photos and to load up on freebies at gifting suites. If it was stuff for the baby, I thought it was fine because we needed whatever we could get. What we didn't need were skateboards and stripper poles and toys for him. He acted as if the world owed him this stuff. He didn't want a real job, because as he would say, "I'd have to work a month for what you can make in one day. Why should I do that?" Hmmm . . . maybe because I just had a baby and wasn't in shape to get back to work?

Once he had walked down the red carpet, there was no

way he was going back to driving talent around on movie sets. That's not what he wanted.

When the wheels were in motion for our reality show, he milked it for all it was worth. He would e-mail companies, tell them about the show, and ask about free stuff we could get from them.

"Don't do that," I said when I caught him. "You can't do that."

"Yeah you can," he responded. "That's what it's all about."

"Don't tell me how to do this business," I replied angrily. "I've been doing this for twenty-three years and you have never done it for a day."

"I've been on the other side of it."

"You spent most of your time sitting in a van. You have no idea how this business works."

Cody and I had always talked about being cool parents. We wanted to be the kind of parents that could have fun and enjoy life, while raising kids that would consider us friends as well as parents. But none of this was enjoyable. There was nothing cool about running around all day, caring for the baby, worrying about bills, and trying to keep my career intact, while he sat around waiting for a million dollars to fall in his lap.

The pressure and anxiety were building up. I needed a drink to take the edge off. About a month after giving birth to Zoie, I had my first glass of wine. Cody and I had a couple of friends over and there was wine for anyone who wanted it. Cody's mom was watching the baby who was sleeping at this point anyway. It seemed harmless. I thought I could use the alcohol as a small release and as long as I wasn't going out to clubs, doing drugs, or partying like I was before, I would be just fine. But the first drink was like every other first drink of mine—calculated and backed by a strong craving. I knew people were coming over. I thought about how I would have that first glass, which, ultimately, led to five glasses. For me, it was so much more than a casual drink at the end of a rough month.

Once I crossed that line, I began drinking every once in a while. Alcohol was welcomed back into my body with open arms. It was only a matter of time before it got ugly.

One night, a few weeks after the first drink, I was under a ton of stress. The level of debt seemed insurmountable, postpartum hormones were turning me into a crazy lady, and on this night, Zoie just wouldn't stop crying. I tried feeding her. I tried changing her. Nothing worked. I was losing my mind. Cody was upstairs helping Mario save the princess (or something like that) and I snapped.

There were times, even during pregnancy, when I would cry myself to sleep because I felt so alone, but I was too frazzled to just sleep it off this time. To ease the pain, I had two glasses of wine, poured the rest of it into a to-go cup, and drove to my friend Melissa's house with Zoie in tow. She always calmed down in the car.

At her house I just lost it. I cried and told Melissa everything. I felt like my life was falling apart. I was filled with uncertainty. Nothing prepares you for diapers and bottles and crying and the lack of sleep that goes along with having a baby. I didn't know how to do this and I felt like I was doing it all by myself. It was not how I pictured a family.

"Am I completely fucking this up?" I thought. "Am I going to completely ruin this kid's life?"

I planned to sleep there so I kept drinking.

Cody noticed I was gone and when he went to the front door he saw one of those strap-on baby holders on the ground outside. It had fallen out of the bag I took with me.

He called me.

"You need to come home right now," he said sternly.

"OK," I said, wiping away the tears.

I went back home we got into a huge screaming match. By that time, I think I had cried all the alcohol out of me. I said some really ugly things. There was truth to all of it, but it didn't come out in a manner that was constructive or that helped the situation or made Cody listen. I had finally opened up about how alone and frustrated I felt, but only because I'd let my guard down by drinking.

When the smoke cleared the next morning, Cody and I went on with our lives as if nothing had happened. I couldn't believe I had driven with Zoie after drinking and I felt terrible. I also knew I had said some awful things to Cody. The huge sense of guilt that was on my shoulders forced me to smooth things over. I told him I didn't mean anything I had said and hung my head in shame.

Cody briefly stepped up his participation in helping with Zoie, but he still didn't have any plans for getting a job. He was concerned about my drinking as well, so I had to hide it. I would make myself a drink every now and then after Zoie went to bed at night and Cody was relaxing in another room. I needed a couple of drinks to take the edge off and I would do whatever it took to have them. If he was there I'd splash some Jack Daniel's into a soda can or pour some vodka into a drink and fill the vodka bottle with water so it looked full.

My parents and his mom came over a lot. Zoie always had a lot of love, but my family saw there was love lost between Cody and me. My mom knew I was drinking on occasion. I called her with my frustrations and she tried to help me.

In August 2008, I went to North Carolina to film a movie called *Port City*. Zoie and I flew but Cody drove across the country to meet us. He was afraid to fly but wanted to be there. It was great to be working again and I really enjoyed my time on set.

Back at the condo where we stayed during filming, Cody was stirring the pot. We were invited to a barbecue with some of the crew members and he couldn't understand why I would want to go.

"You don't make friends with people," he said, acting like he knew everything about "the business."

"Yeah, you do," I replied. "In the environment I grew up working in, we were all a family. That's what happens."

"You're the actor. You can't hang out with the crew."

That's not me at all. He had this elitist view for no reason. When he was a driver on his one job, he talked about how nice Val Kilmer was to everyone and how all the actors loved him, but when the tables were turned he thought, even by association, he was a star. It was so hypocritical. He had tasted a little celebrity in LA and loved it.

At the end of shooting there was an unofficial wrap party. I left Cody behind to watch Zoie. On my own with some of the cast and crew, things got out of control. A bunch of us were drinking inside our trailer, which was conveniently located right in front of a drug dealer's house. Without thinking twice about it, we bought cocaine and started doing lines. I wasn't the instigator as the *National Enquirer* would later report, but I didn't stop anyone from using. It was the first and only time I used drugs since Zoie was born and even as I was doing that first line, I knew it was a huge mistake. But I did it anyway. The addict's rush from the drug was pulsing through my veins. I pushed all of the negative thoughts away and got high.

I did only a few lines so the high didn't last more than a couple of hours. I got back to Cody, who was waiting for me, around 3:00 a.m. Zoie was asleep. Cody was very angry.

"What the hell happened?" he yelled in a whisper.

"Nothing," I said at first, trying to lie.

I came clean about drinking but never told him about the coke. He was still angry. It seemed to me that he was more upset that I went out while he had to watch the baby.

I was extremely disappointed in myself. Using was a horrible thing to do. I didn't want to be that person. I went back to LA with my head down and my relationship on the rocks.

I knew I needed help.

Once I was back home, I was able to stay away from drugs. They weren't easily accessible and I would never bring them into the house with Zoie. Drugs just weren't an option. Alcohol, however, was.

I had a serious problem.

One night at an LA party promoting a new Xbox game, things got bad. I had been drinking during the day which Cody didn't know about. Then we went to dinner with *Full House* creator Jeff Franklin where I drank right in front of Cody. He was pissed. We headed to the event and I drank more. The tension between us escalated.

All the resentment and anger that I had toward him came out. Everything I was still feeling about his not getting a job or helping with the baby came out once again in a cruel, hurtful way. It was the exact same argument that we had had after I left Melissa's house and it led to the same result.

The next morning I apologized, so he assumed that the things I said weren't true. I also made an important decision. No more.

No more drinking, no more lashing out. No more of this dark side that I couldn't control.

I can't have one drink. I can't be a casual drinker. That morning I made a promise to myself that I would do whatever it took to make sure I didn't drink or do drugs ever again. It was the first time that I meant it.

I joined a program and started going to meetings regularly in order to grab ahold of my life before I let my behavior bring me back to where I had been. I could see the pattern forming and it was scary. I didn't want to be that lost person. I couldn't be.

I also thought that if I quit drinking my resentment toward Cody might go away, but I was sober, working the program, taking everything seriously, and the bad relationship was still there. Even with a clear head, I knew it wasn't going to work with him. Once I made the effort to get sober I knew *why* I was drinking again. The relationship was bad and I was drinking to deal with it, not vice versa.

As I got into active recovery, I started making new friends and developing a life outside of my relationship. Cody felt left out. He didn't understand that I needed to do this for myself.

By Halloween, recovery had taken hold of my life. Halloween used to be a drunken, raging nightmare for me. This time, it was fun and simple and easy. Cody and I both had fun together. We took Zoie out for her first Halloween dressed as a pink poodle and she looked adorable. We went to five or six houses with some friends who brought their kids over as well. It was a bright spot in a usually dark relationship.

But I was beginning to realize that I wanted more. I needed that husband and family we had been on Halloween *all* the time, not just on holidays. Cody was never going to be a support for our family. He was never going to be the partner I wanted or deserved. We were in a desperate situation and I finally realized it wasn't going to change—he was never going to pitch in the way I hoped he would.

The person I wanted to grow into—a sober, mature mother—would be stunted as long as I was in this relationship. We weren't growing together and I had to keep growing to stay sober. Either Cody became an active part of our family and my recovery or this marriage had to end.

We got into another one of our usual arguments. It was like that movie *Groundhog Day*—the same fight over and over. I told him to get a job. He told me he had to stay with Zoie and make sure I didn't drink. I didn't need someone to watch over me or a stay-at-home dad when I was barely working myself. The more he used the excuse of needing to watch over me, the more I tried to isolate myself from him. He wasn't helping. He was creating an uncomfortable living environment and I needed to get out.

After the latest blowout, I went to my parents' house and stayed there for a couple of days with Zoie. When I came back, we never talked about the argument or my days away. It was the giant pink elephant in the room and we weren't saying anything to resolve it or to move forward. Nothing had changed. I knew, for sure, that this wasn't going to work.

On November 18, I left for good after fighting about the same old thing once again.

"I'm leaving," I shouted. "I need to go to my parents'."

"You're not taking Zoie," he said, wrapping his arms around her. "You're not taking my daughter."

"I'm just going to take her to my parents' for a couple of days," I replied calmly. "I'll bring her back. There is no way I would not have you see your daughter. Whatever happens with us, I'm not going to take you away from her."

He didn't care. He picked her up and told me I wasn't taking her.

"Yeah, I am," I said.

He was holding her and I wasn't going to grab her out of his arms. I didn't know what to do.

"Are you going to take the dog this time?" he said. The last time I'd stayed with my parents, I had left Ginger, the Yorkie Shaun bought me once upon a time, with him.

"Yes, I'm taking Ginger."

"You can leave, but you're not taking Zoie," he repeated. "And good luck having a judge grant an ex–drug addict any custody. I'm going to get full custody, and you're not going to get any time with her."

I was horrified.

I left the house and called my attorney, who said I couldn't leave with my daughter because if I did and Cody went for full custody, he could use that against me. I went back to the house. Cody and I didn't talk; we just orbited each other.

He went outside and I got ready to head to a recovery meeting. I had a bag packed for me and for Zoie. I called my mom and told her what was going on and when I got off, I knew what I had to do. I knew I would share Zoie and he wouldn't. I knew this was my chance to take her to my parents' and work everything out from there. I put Zoie in her car seat, grabbed my dog Ginger, and took off.

I saw him as I pulled out.

"Hey, see you later," he said, thinking I was off to a meeting. I waved and that was that. I pulled out of the gates and called my mom.

"I did it," I said, trembling. "I left. I have the baby and I left."

I think her exact response was, "Oh, shit."

Cody sent me a text later that night asking what was going on, but I didn't respond because I didn't know what to say. The next day I filed the papers for separation.

Deciding to be happy has been one of the hardest decisions I've ever had to make. For much of my adult life I have consciously chosen to be unhappy—to stay in miserable situations or do things that brought me only heartache. I put what I knew would make me happy and healthy aside. Making the choice to be happy, as weird as it sounds, is much tougher.

chapter twenty-two

THE FIGHT OF MY LIFE

i knew I had made the right decision the second I left, but filing for divorce was just the first step in creating the happiness I wanted for Zoie and me. Two days after filing, I took off my wedding ring. I admit it felt strange to be doing that for the second time at twenty-six years old. But when that ring comes off, you realize that it's really over. No matter how sure I was about the decision, I was still sad.

The fallout that followed reminds me every day that it was the right decision.

My first divorce was incredibly peaceful. We had a mediator, we hugged, and that was it. It was as pleasant as a divorce could be—no fighting, no publicity stunts, nothing but respect for each other.

This divorce, I'd soon discover, was a totally different story.

Cody was furious and he was going to do whatever it took to get back at me for leaving him. He started by going on the Internet and talking to reporters about the time I drove drunk with Zoie. I was wrong for doing that and I regret it more than anyone can imagine, but I was disappointed that he went running to the tabloids. He also did a story with *Us Weekly* where he talked about our sex life. It was tasteless but I wasn't surprised; even when we were together he was looking to sell a story to make a quick buck. I still hoped he would take Zoie's best interests into consideration.

I knew he loved her but I wasn't sure whether he was really motivated by what he thought was best for Zoie, or if he just wanted to hurt me and push me into using so that he could win custody of her. Clearly, he was trying to push my buttons by creating a public battle over what I felt was a private matter.

I think Cody wanted me to feel as heartbroken as he felt, so he ran to the media and stabbed me in the back. Although I think he truly did love me, it's hard to respect someone who tells you that and then sells his stories and our private, intimate moments to a weekly tabloid.

Because of his antics, I had paparazzi following me to lunch and sitting outside my parents' home where I moved with Zoie after the split. I had dealt with bad publicity before, but I never had photographers stalk me, appearing out of nowhere, like I did now—not even after I was just out of rehab. I think they wait until you are at your toughest, lowest point before they decide to make you a target.

The battle moved to the courtroom. Cody wanted full custody of Zoie. As he promised the night I left, he was going to do whatever it took to take my baby from me.

It was heartbreaking and incredibly stressful. Under normal circumstances I would give up. I would start to drink, turn to drugs, and free myself from all the horrible feelings.

This time though, I was working harder than ever to stay sober. I was going to meetings three or four times a week, talking to my sober friends regularly, and working on my recovery as hard as possible.

I also focused on my Zoie. She's what mattered most, so during the hardest of times I focused on the positive things in my life and on what I wanted for her and for me. I didn't let my anger toward other people or at the situations I couldn't control lead me back to drinking and using.

Something as simple as just talking about my feelings, which I've never done in my life, kept me sane. Before, I kept my feelings to myself and pretended that everything was OK. Now, I opened up and even when I didn't know what to say—when I wanted to throw something, kick a wall, cry and laugh all at the same time—I had the right people around me to help me through the hard times. I let my guard down and opened myself up to weakness. And there was strength in that.

I was focused on the first step of recovery—admitting that you are powerless over alcohol. I was starting to truly understand what it meant to say that I could control only the choices I made. If I chose to drink, all bets were off; I wouldn't know where that would lead or what I would end up doing. It was a chance I could no longer take.

Every day was a battle and the temptation was still there. That's what alcoholism and drug addiction are—obsessions of the mind and an allergy of the body. Over time, it gets easier, but during this first real attempt at sobriety, it was very hard. There are bad days even now, when I think, "If I could only have a liter of Jack Daniel's and an eight ball of coke . . ." That's when I pick up my phone and instead of calling my dealer, I call my friends. I tell them how I'm feeling and we talk it through.

I'm not perfect. That was an equally hard lesson to learn. In December, I made a mistake. I returned to North Carolina—the place of my last big breakdown—to film a new movie called *Redefining Love*. I was in a situation that I should have avoided, but didn't. I went out with a few friends from the film and had a few drinks.

This time, though, was different. I knew instantly that it was so wrong. The rush was gone. It just wasn't working for me anymore. I did it because I was on autopilot, but it didn't even feel good. For the first time, it didn't feel like a solution to anything. It wasn't me anymore. It was like putting on a suit that didn't fit. It used to look good on me but now it just wasn't my style.

I went back to my hotel room and freaked out. I was so angry at myself. I called my sober friends for support. It was a painful, emotional, lying-on-the-floor, crying-my-eyes-out night. There was nothing enjoyable about the drinking experience.

But there was one positive I latched on to: I stopped myself before the drinking had gone any further. I was in North Carolina. I knew exactly where to get drugs, but I didn't. I was drinking to loosen up, feel interesting, and cure all those old insecurities, but I stopped myself. I may have taken a step back, but when I didn't make that leap to losing control, I also took a step forward.

I had to restart my sobriety clock, which was devastating. I'm glad it was miserable—hitting bottom was so painful I knew I never wanted to go back there. After all the bad times and near-death experiences, having a few drinks felt like the worst experience yet.

When I returned to LA, I was back in court fighting for the right to be a mother. Cody questioned my past and the judge ordered an emergency investigation into my life to determine whether I was an unfit mother.

This was right after I had slipped in North Carolina, and I was frightened. I know I've made mistakes, and I know I haven't been perfect, but I'm a good mom. I love my daughter more than anything. I was honest about what happened in North Carolina and it was proven that I was not a danger to Zoie.

The court did order, however, that for the time being, I couldn't take Zoie anywhere without my parents being there. Living with my parents was a good thing. It was what I needed until I felt a bit stronger. I needed the love and family support they gave me, and they were happy to spend a lot of time with Zoie.

My dad was playing with Zoie one day when he looked at

me and said, "You know, Jodie, your mom and I love this little baby so much. There was a day when we thought this would never happen, that we would never have a grandbaby. This means so much to us and I just want to let you know that."

Hearing that meant so much to me and at the same time it made me sad to think that there was a time in my life when my parents had resigned themselves to thinking that I would probably die before having a family. It was a bitter-sweet moment.

It was frustrating that a judge wanted me supervised, but I was willing to do whatever it took to show that I deserved to take care of her. Have people watch over me. Fine. Drug test me. Do it. I have nothing to hide anymore. I'm a good mom and I will do whatever it takes to prove it.

Even as I write this, I'm still battling for the right to share custody and attempting to peacefully end my marriage. Through all of this, I have had a great support group. I have my parents and I have the kind of friends that I can call at any hour of the day to talk about what's bothering me. I can go lie on their couch and cry for hours, saying nothing at all. Accepting that I need these caring people in my life doesn't mean I'm a weak person. I don't have to be OK all the time. It took me my whole life to learn that, to understand that no one is happy all the time, no one is perfect.

A real rehab program is a very spiritual process. We have to believe that a power greater than ourselves can restore us to sanity. You can't do the program effectively without God or some sort of higher power in your life. It just doesn't work. I definitely have a newfound spiritual view of life. Even when

I was using, I had an interest in spirituality and have relied on that at some rough moments in my life. So for me to believe in a higher power while sober is a lot easier. I'm finding myself and learning that what I have to offer this world as a sober person is good enough.

Recovery is a tough road, but this time I'm committed. Some people can get it right the first time and never have to go back, and some people keep beating their heads against the wall over and over again. I may have fallen at times, but I always get up. I know what I need to do and I'm making it happen.

For now there is only one love in my life and that's Zoie. She will always be that light at the end of the tunnel. Having her and being her mom is my saving grace. No matter what else falls apart, I know I have that and I always will.

When I'm with her I'm in Zoieland, this incredible place in life. The responsibilities began the day she was born but it took time for me to grow into being a parent. It didn't happen overnight.

As time goes on, there are all kinds of "firsts," the good ones and the bad ones. I've started to come into my own as a mother. My maternal instincts have just sort of taken over. When Zoie got her first cold, I handled it like a champ and so did she. She hated the little snot-sucker thing, but she was good with the pediatrician. I just tried to stay calm and eventually the cold went away.

When she started crawling, she'd bump her head on the table and I would look at her and say, "You're OK," and she'd just keep doing what she was doing. She trusted me.

From the beginning I've tried to talk to her like a person. I know she doesn't understand my words, but I think she deserves that. I tell her what I'm doing as I'm doing it. "Mommy is making you a bottle," "Mommy is cleaning up." I'll sing to her or read her a book.

Zoie loves Elmo and especially Barney. There are Barney songs that haunt me in my sleep, but because Zoie loves them, I sit and let my brain turn to purple mush.

Every day with Zoie is a blessing. At twenty-seven, I have the energy and the spunk to be a great young mother. I'm proud of her and our mother-daughter relationship. She's my greatest accomplishment. I love teaching her new things and watching her grow. I am proud to take her to a grocery store or out to lunch with friends. She's perfect and I always feel "Yep, that's mine!"

One afternoon, I was playing with Zoie, rolling around on the ground and making faces, and I realized that there is nowhere else in the world that I would rather be. There's not one club or one drink or one person I'd rather be with. Her little giggle is the best high.

She gives me a sense of great joy. When she's in her stroller playing with a toy, I'll watch her and feel overcome that she's just a little person in a big, big world—and that it's up to me to take care of her and protect her. I truly cherish that responsibility and I'm blessed to have the opportunity.

I have overlooked many blessings in the past. Now, I'm hoping to get to a place where I realize these gifts—and I'm getting there more each day—and take advantage of them. I'm piecing my life together, changing how I want the picture to look. I don't know what that picture is right now, what the happy rainbows, pretty flowers, and pink poodles will be, but I know that I'll get there.

And even when I arrive, I know something will come up that will challenge me—something heart-wrenching or emotional—but I will try to remember that no matter how bad something is, or how great, it's not going to last. That's OK. Now, I'm trying to handle life on life's terms and not be rigid about what I expect. I have to just deal with what life hands me and make the most out of it.

It may seem as though I have a lot standing in my way— financial issues, a pending divorce, a custody battle, and a fight for sobriety. But even with all of that on my shoulders, I feel better. In the past, when all my troubles were buried under my addictions, things looked great on the outside but on the inside I was a wreck. But I now know that happiness isn't about the events going on in your life; it's about how you handle them. It's about falling down and standing up straighter than you did before. It's about realizing that nothing comes easy.

Life isn't like a *Full House* episode. Uncle Jesse isn't going to come into that courtroom and convince the judge to rule in my favor by singing a Beach Boys song. There isn't going to be an easy out to every conflict. There is no milkman or paperboy or evening TV. There are good moments and bad moments and not everything will tie together nicely in the end. But that's life, and I think I'm finally starting to get it.

A LETTER TO ZOIE

To my little Zo-bug,

I know you can't even read this yet, but someday you'll be able to and I hope you feel the love in every word. You are my angel, my light, and the most beautiful thing I have ever seen. Each day that I get to spend with you makes me feel more joy than I ever thought possible. There are so many hopes and dreams that I hold for your life; whatever they turn out to be, you will have my support.

Please know that I am doing my best at any given moment for you. I am not perfect, but perfection does not make a parent. Love does. Love is wanting something more for someone else than you do for yourself. It is being able to put your needs aside so that someone else (for me, that's you) always gets the best. It is admitting that you sometimes have no idea what you're doing but you're willing to try even when it's scary. I pray that I will show you all of these things and more.

You are the most important and amazing thing I have ever done with my life. There is no greater success that I could ever come close to than having you. You are perfection in every sense of the word. As I watch you sleep in your crib, or discover something new in the world, or laugh at me making a silly face, I know what God looks like. And I am blessed to have you.

I have made lots of mistakes in my life, some very painful and tragic ones for sure. I pray that you don't have to go through any of these things for yourself. But as every parent knows, I can tell you what to do but it doesn't mean you'll listen. Just ask your grandparents, they know all too well! Someday you will come to a decision in your life when you need a friend and someone who will listen without judgment. I am ALWAYS here for you. There is nothing you can say or ever do to make me not love you. You have my heart and there is no way I can ever get it back, nor would I want to.

If I could imagine your life for you it would be easy, with no heartbreak or turmoil. No tough lessons to learn and nothing to stop you from your dreams. But I know that is totally unrealistic and foolish. Whether you fall and skin your knee, get a bad grade in school, or have your heart broken Mommy is here for you.

People have told me about the "mama bear" that comes out when you have a child of your own, that you would die for your baby in an instant. I now know that they weren't lying at all! There is nothing in the world that would stop me from giving everything in my life for you. I am absolutely in love with you!

One of the hardest things that I know you will have to deal with is that Mommy and Daddy aren't together. This adds some extra challenges to your life. As you grow up there will be some confusion. Please know that we both love you. I hope that we can be there for you as parents who love you and want the best for you regardless of what has gone on between us. On both sides of the family, you have grandparents, aunties, and uncles who absolutely adore you! I wish that this didn't have to be this way, but I know that you will be able to make it through being so loved and cherished.

Most important, I hope you grow into a woman who loves herself. It is not an easy thing, self-love. It takes lots of practice and time. But as a woman who is learning how to get there herself, I hope I can give that gift to you as you grow.

Zoie, you are everything to me. You give me strength and courage that I couldn't find in myself. You have shown me how easy it can be to laugh. And you have shown me that life really is amazing. Thank you. You are the wisest teacher I've ever met and I continue to learn from your beautiful little spirit every day. I love you, I love you, I love you.

Love,
Your Mommy

ACKNOWLEDGMENTS

Writing this book was one of the hardest, most honest things I've ever done in my life. Without the support of those around me whom I love and who love me back, I don't think I could have done it.

There are so many people that I want to thank, that I can't even begin to write them all down. First and foremost, I would like to thank my parents. Mom, Dad—I don't even have the words to describe how much I love you, appreciate you, and respect you. Now that I am a mom, I'm beginning to understand that type of unconditional love and I've really put yours to the test. Thank you for always being there. You have saved my life and I am so lucky to have you both.

I would also like to thank my Zoie, of course! I wrote you a whole letter in this book, just so you can have a small idea of how much I love you.

Special thanks are in order for my entire sober family who recently blessed my life. You have all saved my ass on more than one occasion and I am eternally grateful. You are there for me whenever I need you and you made writing this book an easier step to take. I have so many names that I could put down, but I don't want to break any anonymity. You know who you are, and you know that I love you! Thank you for teaching me how to live in my own skin.

To my writer, Jon Warech, you helped me put my life on paper and have it all make sense! I couldn't have done this without you. It was a pleasure writing this with you. I wouldn't have wanted to do it with anyone else.

I would also like to thank Endeavor's Kirby Kim, as well as Simon Spotlight Entertainment editor Sarah Sper, publisher Jen Bergstrom, Publicity Director Jen Robinson, and Art Director Michael Nagin.

Jon Warech would also like to thank the team at Simon Spotlight Entertainment: editor Sarah Sper, publisher Jen Bergstrom, Publicity Director Jen Robinson, and Art Director Michael Nagin. A special thanks also goes out to Endeavor's Kirby Kim, grandmother/publicist Joy Warech, mom, dad, Katie, and his entire family, Victoria Van Bell, Justin Smith, Ryan Smiths (both of them), Joshua Alhalel, Matt Cooper, Katie Rhames, The Einhorn Family for Season 1 on DVD, Ted Spiker and the entire journalism department at the University of Florida, and Tim Tebow for making it impossible to work on Saturdays.